21 DEADLY MISTAKES

Gun Tactics Which Could Kill You

by

Guy Hargreaves

Copyright 2014 by Guy Hargreaves

All rights reserved. No part of this publication may be reproduced, stored in a retrieval system or transmitted, in any form, or by any means, electronic, mechanical, recorded, photocopied, or otherwise, without the prior written permission of the copyright owner of this book, except by a reviewer who may quote brief passages in a review.

The scanning, uploading, and distribution of this book via the Internet or via any other means without the permission of the publisher is illegal and punishable by law. Please purchase only authorized electronic editions and do not participate in or encourage electronic piracy of copy written materials.

All products, photos or mention of products and links or website addresses in this book are used with the express written consent of their owners. Except where expressly noted, the use of these product names, examples, photos or website links does not constitute a recommendation of these products. The author and publisher advise readers to take full responsibility for their safety and know their limits. Before practicing the skills described in this book, be sure that your equipment is well maintained, and do not take risks beyond your level of experience, aptitude, training, and comfort level.

First Edition: June 2015
Second Edition: November 2017
Printed in the United States of America

Table of Contents

INTRODUCTION	i
RULE 1	1
Preparation & Safety	
RULE 2	7
The Warrior Mindset	
RULE 3	15
Take Advantage Of Cover, If It Is Available	
RULE 4	23
The Triangle Of Gunfight Survival	
RULE 5	29
Target Acquisition	
RULE 6	33
Stress And The Unarmed Suspect Can Be A Killer	
RULE 7	39
"Flinch" Will Destroy Your Accuracy	
RULE 8	43
Firearms Shooting Fundamentals	
RULE 9	55
Weapon Advantage	
RULE 10	67
Tombstone Courage, The "Dirty Harry Syndrome"	
RULE 11	71
Neer Give Up The Fight Or Your Gun	

RULE 12	75
Proper Distance	
RULE 13	79
Reliability Of Weapons & Equipment	
RULE 14	83
Handgun And Caliber Selection	
RULE 15	93
Proper Holster Selection	
RULE 16	105
Never Assume Anything	
RULE 17	115
The 21-foot Rule	
RULE 18	119
Don't Underestimate The Threat Of Females And The Elderly	
RULE 19	123
Don't Rely On Less Lethal Options	
RULE 20	131
Modern Technology Makes Bullet Proof Equipment Very Effective	
RULE 21	133
Relaxing Too Soon	
CASE EXAMPLE	137
Why You Should Never Relax And Not Be Vigilant With Stalkers	
SUMMARY	141
The 21 Deadly Rules Of Gunfight Survival	
CLOSING COMMENTS	147

Introduction

WITH GUNS WE ARE CITIZENS, WITHOUT THEM WE ARE SUBJECTS.

When armed terrorists attacked the Charlie Hebdo headquarters in Paris over Muhammad cartoons on January 7, 2015, unarmed police officers were forced to flee for their lives. The BBC reported the Paris gunmen killed 12 in their attack on the Charlie Hebdo headquarters; that number included eight journalists, two unarmed French police officers, a caretaker and a visitor. When armed terrorists attacked people gathered in Garland, Texas, on May 3, 2015, over Prophet Muhammad cartoons, a single armed Texas police officer cut them down and no innocent citizens or police were killed. The difference between the Garland and Paris terrorist attacks can be summed up in one word: guns.

Law-abiding citizens in the U.S. use guns to defend themselves against criminals as many as 2.5 million times every year — or about 6,850 times a day. This means that each year, firearms are used 80 times more often to protect the lives of honest citizens, than to take lives. Of the 2.5 million times citizens use their guns to defend themselves every year, the overwhelming majority merely brandish their gun or fire a warning shot to scare off their attackers. Less than 8% of the time, a citizen will kill or wound his/her attacker. Even anti-gun researchers concede that guns are used at least 1.5 million times annually for self-defense. A survey of male felons in 11 state prisons dispersed across the U.S. found 69% personally knew other criminals who had been "scared off, shot at, wounded, or captured by an armed victim".

Some of the extreme gun control advocates in this country promote the idea that America is the "murder capital of the world", and that guns are responsible for this epidemic. The pseudo intellectual proponents of this propaganda consider themselves to be morally superior. They ammo up their rhetorical arsenal with psychosexual references to the "dangerous gun culture" of the United States, promoting the idea America has a sick and twisted obsession with firearms. The reality of official crime statistics prove they obviously have an agenda in conflict with the truth, and prove they are attempting to utilize emotion and false information to bring their ideal of an unarmed, law-abiding American citizen to fruition. Do not be fooled by this propaganda, which is alien from the truth. It is true that the U.S. has the highest number of "mass shootings" of any country in the world, but it is the overall homicide rate which is more important. Wouldn't you think that you would be safer to live in a country which has the highest "mass shooting" incidents in the world (U.S.) than a country like Mexico which has 5 times the homicide rate overall per capita. All you have to do to discredit this propaganda is to look at the worldwide homicide statistics. The data shows the United States has a lower homicide rate per capita than the majority of the countries in the world.

It is true that America has, by far, more guns per capita than any other nation on the face of this planet (90 guns per every 100 U.S. citizens). The U.S. is even far ahead of Serbia, which is 2nd in world statistics with 58 guns for every 100 Serbian citizens. What they do not tell you is that the United States is not even close to being the "murder capitol of the world". In fact, the United States is not even in the top 100 countries in the world for homicides per capita. The U.S. is 111th, the bottom 50%, of the 218 nations surveyed. (See the United Nations Office of Drugs and Crime[UNODC] "Global Study on Homicide 2013" statistics for homicide rates worldwide.)

These statistics clearly show that it is the number of criminals, not guns, which determines the violent crime rate for your country. It is noted that the city of Detroit, which has some of the toughest gun control laws in the United States, would be #2 in the world for homicide statistics per capita, if Detroit were a country instead of part of the United States. The socialist and strict gun control nation of Honduras is #1 in the world homicide ratings with a 90.4 homicides per 100,000 inhabitants. The *2012 List Of Countries By Intentional Homicide Rate* per year, per 100,000 inhabitants, shows the strict gun control nation of Mexico has 21.5 homicides per 100,000, while the U.S. has only 4.7 homicides per 100,000 inhabitants.

In 1971, Article 10 of the present Mexico Constitution was reformed to limit the *right to keep arms* within the home only, and reserved the *right to bear arms* outside the home, only to those explicitly authorized by law (i.e. police, military, armed security officers). The following year, the *Mexican Federal Law of Firearms and Explosives* came into force and gave the federal government complete jurisdiction and control of the legal proliferation of firearms in the country; at the same time, heavily limiting and restricting the legal access to firearms by civilians. As a result of the changes, openly carrying a firearm in public is virtually forbidden to private citizens, unless explicitly authorized by the Secretariat of National Defense (SEDENA). For purposes of personal protection, firearms in Mexico are only permitted within the place of residence of the Mexican citizen and only the type and caliber permitted by Mexican law.

In contrast, the nation of Switzerland has one of the highest gun ownership rates in the world, but an extremely low 2012 homicide rate of only 0.6 per 100,000 inhabitants. In addition, the vast majority of Swiss men between the ages of 20 and 30 are conscripted into the militia and undergo military training, including weapons training. The personal weapons (including military assault rifles) of the militia are kept at their homes. A December 20, 2012 issue of TIME magazine stated, "Switzerland trails behind only the U.S., Yemen, and Serbia in the number of guns per capita. Weapons are kept at home because of the long- held belief that enemies could invade tiny Switzerland quickly, so every soldier had to be able to fight his way to his regiment's assembly point. (Switzerland was at risk of being invaded by Germany during World War II but was spared, historians say, because every Swiss man was armed and trained to shoot.)"

Right-to-carry laws in many states of the U.S. permit individuals who meet certain "minimally restrictive" criteria (such as completion of a background check and gun safety course) to carry concealed firearms in most public places. The vast majority of U.S. states now permit right-to-carry, but statistics from previous years show right-to-carry states experienced a violent crime rate 24% lower than the rest of the U.S., a murder rate which was 28% lower, and a robbery rate 50% lower than states which did not allow concealed carry permits. U.S. crime statistics reflect armed citizens frequently kill more crooks than do the police. In some years past, law-abiding, armed citizens shot and killed at least twice as many criminals as police, even though most receive very little training to prepare them for these potential deadly force encounters.

I have been a law enforcement officer most of my life. Civilian gunfights almost always happen by surprise. In home defense situations, there is sometimes a warning that a threat is imminent. You may have dogs that bark or an alarm system, but daytime threats at the local convenience store, the bank, the gas station, or in that bad neighborhood where you were forced to stop for a red light, can appear from anywhere at any moment. Now that you know the real official statistics, let me tell you a short story about why I decided to write this book. Larry, a 67 year old dentist living in Topeka, Kansas, recently called me and related a story about the apprehension of a burglar on his property which nearly cost him his life. On Dec. 6, 2011, Larry heard his wife and friend scream for help from the small rental cottage behind his home. The cottage is located only a few yards from his residence., He immediately became suspicious that a burglary was taking place. Jumping up from his computer and retrieving his Colt Maverick .380 Auto, he called 911 while running out toward the sound of their screams. His wife and renter had walked in on a burglary in progress. From that point on, Larry made some serious mistakes and he's lucky to be alive. Larry was raised on a farm in rural Kansas and had handled firearms his entire life, even as a very young man. He was also an avid collector, a big and small game hunter, who considered himself extremely proficient due to his many years of hunting experience, and a three-year tour overseas in the US Army. But facing a career criminal, just out of prison with a 30 year history of crime and violence and access to a high capacity 9mm Glock was a different situation.

Larry instinctively charged through the front entrance of the cottage into a darker room, silhouetting himself to the criminal. He then pointed the Colt at him, calling him to show his hands and get down on the floor. Larry was immediately confronted by a stocky white male burglar who had recently been released from prison. Larry was now within 6 feet of this burglar who could have easily grabbed his weapon. When the burglar did not comply, Larry squeezed the trigger several times on the Colt pistol, but nothing happened. The weapon would not fire! Larry, under extreme stress, became frantic while trying to assess why the pistol wouldn't discharge. Under duress, he simply had forgotten to disengage the safety. The burglar had one of his hands in his pocket. Larry suspected he might have a hidden weapon in that pocket when the burglar refused to show his hands. At this point Larry smashed the burglar in the face with his fist... and that's when the fight started.

Fortunately for Larry, his brother Bruce (a former prison guard and burly truck driver) entered right behind him to help. He put the burglar in a chokehold and pulled him to the ground while Larry continued hitting him. Larry spied a wine bottle on the counter and smashed the burglar on the skull with the wine bottle to end the struggle. Larry did not qualify as a pistol expert that day, but he did get an excellent qualification as an ace wine bottle swinger. The case later went to trial and the burglar will now be in prison until he is about 75 years old. The burglar had earlier stolen a 9mm Glock from the cottage, but fortunately for Larry, this loaded pistol had already been carried to the burglar's escape vehicle prior to Larry's arrival on the scene. This story had a happy ending but could have easily resulted in the very tragic death of Larry. Would you have responded in the same fashion as Larry? What mistakes, if any, do you think Larry made in this potential life and death confrontation?

Larry is an intelligent and well-educated man who usually has good common sense, but made four significant errors (violation of RULES #3, #6, #10, and #12) that you will read about in this book. RULE #3 deals with taking advantage of cover when you are involved in a potential gunfight. Why run into the cottage and silhouette yourself to the criminal in the doorway for an easy shot? Why not wait outside and take cover behind a tree where you expose a very small target to your adversary when he exits the location?

RULE #6 deals with stress. You need to develop muscle memory that makes shooting your firearm an instinctive reaction via extensive training. If you have to think about it, you might hesitate and hesitation means possible freezing under stress. Under extreme stress, Larry forgot to take the safety off on his pistol. Larry did not train in shooting his new pistol, which led to his failure to release the safety switch when he was under stress. Under stress you will revert to your lowest level of training.

Semi-automatic pistols may be superior to revolvers in magazine capacity, but you are probably better off with a revolver if you are not an avid shooter who practices on a regular basis and knows how to respond to a weapon malfunction with a semi-auto pistol. Revolvers do not usually have a safety you need to remember to disengage. Ironically, several months prior to this incident, Larry had asked me what type of handgun I would recommend for home security. I suggested he purchase a .410 caliber Taurus Judge or Smith & Wesson Governor revolver since they are simple to operate and have much better stopping power than a .380 caliber semi-auto pistol that might jam. Unfortunately, Larry disregarded my advice and purchased a small semi-auto with a safety mechanism, on which he had not been trained. Although I am certain Larry will never again forget about the safety issue, he now carries a revolver. The importance of this book is to provide you with some common sense practical knowledge that even some highly trained law enforcement officers often forget during the extreme stress of a life and death encounter.

RULE #10 is the "Dirty Harry" syndrome, sometimes called Tombstone Courage. Don't develop the "Dirty Harry" syndrome and try to be the Lone Ranger. Larry was smart enough not to enter the cottage alone, which may have saved his life, but why not wait for the police to show up? No amount of stolen property is worth risking your life for!

RULE #12 deals with "Proper Distance". Maintain proper distance to keep your weapon out of reach of your adversary. Distance is usually in your favor, especially if you are a small female confronting a large male suspect. Never forget that 8% to 10% of the trained police officers killed in the line of duty, were killed with their own guns, when the unarmed suspects managed to wrestle their pistols away from them. I do not tell this story to embarrass Larry, but to show that the rules and tactics contained in this book are sometimes far more important to save your life than your accuracy with a firearm. Larry is an excellent shot, but did not use good tactics, except for the quick thinking to grab the wine bottle when his pistol didn't work.

In America today, we now have a larger percentage of civilians carrying firearms than at any time in U.S. history. The purpose of this book is to educate the law-abiding general public on some of the more important rules to remember to survive a deadly force encounter. There are many misconceptions concerning the techniques of armed self-defense. The simple possession of a handgun does not always scare off bad guys. Most law enforcement officers are thoroughly trained with numerous officer survival courses and should have a thorough knowledge of the legal, tactical and mental preparation aspects required to survive a gunfight, but the average citizen who owns a firearm has no, or little training, on how to survive a deadly force encounter. Nonetheless, the survival rules outlined in this book are also a good reminder to every police officer of some of the common sense mistakes we can all make when under the stress of a life and death encounter.

The armed citizen who is a Concealed Carry Permit (CCP) holder usually has some marksmanship and safety training, but rarely, if ever, receives any practical tactical training guidelines on how to respond or prepare for a myriad of potential deadly force scenarios. There are many high quality firearms familiarization, safety, and accuracy training courses available to the general public, but this book will provide you with 21 important deadly force survival rules which may prove to be more important to your survival, and the survival of your loved ones, than your accuracy with a firearm or any information you would probably receive from a general one day gun safety or CCP training course.

The average American citizen mistakenly assumes that all you need is a gun and good marksmanship to protect yourself and your family, but have you really thought in detail about exactly if, when, and how you would react when someone is threatening your family or breaking into your home? Many American citizens would respond, "Well, if they break into my house I will just shoot them!" Do you know there are states in the U.S. in which you cannot legally utilize deadly force in a burglary unless you have retreated to a far corner or bedroom in your home and the burglar is still coming at you with criminal intent which puts you in fear of your life? Have you developed any plans of how to respond to someone breaking into your home? Will you hesitate to fire your gun because you do not know if you can legally use your weapon? Will you have your weapon taken away from you because you waited to draw your weapon until the suspect was already on top of you and wrestling the weapon away from you? If you hesitate or freeze because you don't know how, or if you will be capable, of responding, your firearm could prove to be a detriment, not an asset, and result in your demise. If this is the case, you should consider the purchase of a non-lethal TASER®, conducted electrical weapon, for your protection.

When you come home and find your house broken into, do you immediately rush into your house to see what is stolen, only to find the burglar is still in your home? If you are not smart enough to stay outside and call the police for back up before you enter your home, you might lose more than property; you open yourself up to become the victim of a rape, assault or murder. I could write an entire encyclopedia about the potential "what if" scenarios you may possibly encounter, but in all probability you would not remember all the details of that extensive list in a stressful situation. In the military, they try to exercise the KISS principle (Keep It Simple Stupid). They know that under life and death stress situations, soldiers respond based on training, and simple concepts are easier to remember. I have; therefore, decided to provide you with a list of 21 simple rules which should be easy for you to remember and could save your life.

I start this book with a disclaimer; I am not providing legal advice on how to respond to life-threatening situations which may require a deadly force response. I am not an attorney and this book is not intended to provide legal guidance to police officers or civilians with a Concealed Carry Permit (CCP). Every state in the United States has different laws with regard to the legal utilization of deadly force and I would strongly suggest you make yourself completely aware of those laws for your state of residence prior to carrying a firearm. Some states allow the utilization of deadly force when a criminal is in the imminent commission of property crimes such as arson and burglary, but I would strongly advise against the use of deadly force in property crime situations, unless you are threatened and in fear of your life. No valuables are worth risking a criminal indictment. I always recommend that the use of deadly force should only be applied when you are in fear of your life, or to save the life of another innocent citizen. If you find yourself in fear for your life, you need training to prepare to respond without hesitation. Although I do not give legal advice, I do know it is always better to be judged by twelve peers, than carried by six pallbearers.

For example, a woman in Ohio used her gun to ward off an abduction in August 2014 while she was out walking her dog. Although she was licensed to carry a gun for some time, she had only recently actually started carrying one for protection. While she was out walking her dog, on a path near an elementary school in Lancaster, Ohio, two men approached her with a baseball bat and threatened to abduct her. They literally came out of the woods and told her "You're coming with us!" Her dog provided no defense in deterring the men, but she slipped her gun out of a pocket. "As I was doing that the other gentleman came toward me and raised the baseball bat." She responded by aiming the gun at them and stated, "I have this and I'm not afraid to use it." The men backed off and left the location. Ohio has experienced a massive surge of new concealed carry permit requests. According to the Columbus Dispatch newspaper, 96,972 new concealed carry permits were issued in 2013, a 50 percent increase from 2012.

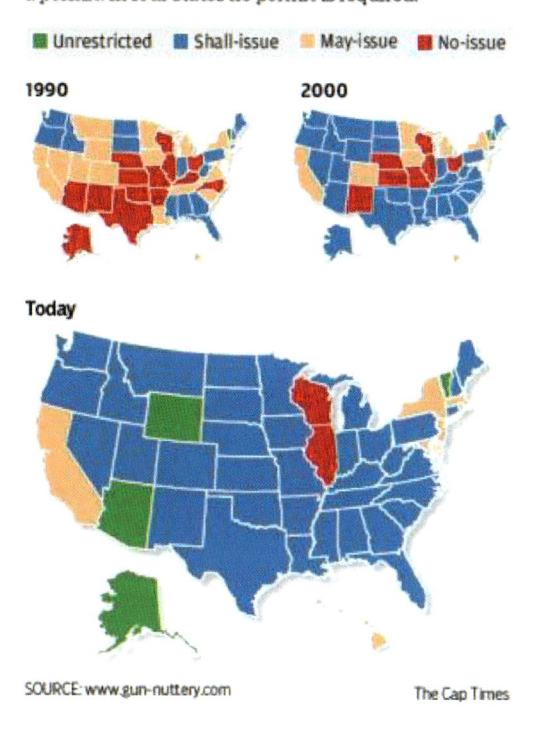

Bottom map for year 2010

The U.S. violent crime rate has decreased over 49% since 1991, but is still a significant concern in our society. Many law-abiding citizens realize they may need to come to their own defense and cannot rely solely on the police or security guards. In some regions of our country, it may take 20 minutes or longer before the police can respond to a violent crime. Many U.S. citizens therefore prudently decide it might be wise to have access to firearms and many of them obtain a Concealed Carry Permit (CCP) to protect their loved ones in the event the police are not available to respond immediately.

There are many highly talented firearm instructors and organizations available to provide general firearm safety and accuracy courses to the general public. The National Rifle Association (NRA) provides some excellent pistol safety and accuracy training courses for as little as $150, but there are few specific gunfight survival training programs available to the general public.

Courses on gunfight tactics, mindset, judgment, utilization of cover, and officer survival techniques, are generally only available to law enforcement and the military. The purpose of this book is to provide some of that type of specialized knowledge to the law- abiding citizen who is a CCP holder. You will see by reading the 21 rules of gunfight survival in this book, that firearms accuracy is only one of the three corners of the survival triangle which decides who will survive, and who will perish in a gunfight.

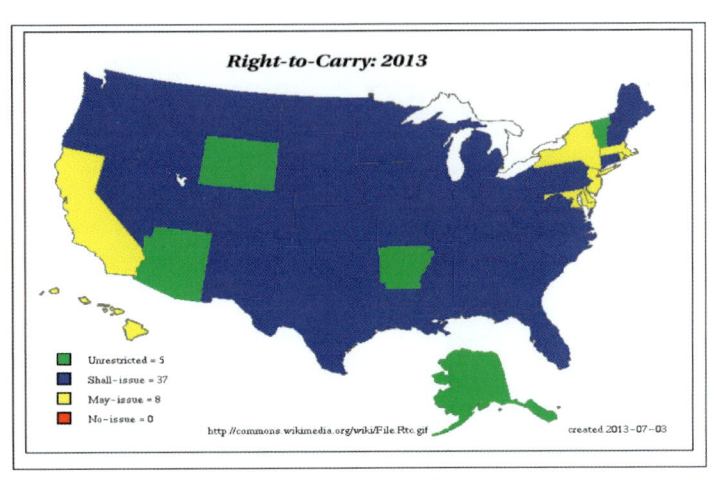

US Right to carry per state for year 2013

I was initially reticent to provide the information contained in this book to the general public, for fear it would eventually also come into the hands of the violent predators, until I spoke with several of my law enforcement colleagues who laughed when I expressed this concern and stated, "Are you kidding? It is the law- abiding citizens, that 'civilian sheepdog' you talk about, who need this knowledge more than anyone." The violent predators, who are like wolves, spend their entire lives training to be better killers. The prisons are nothing more than an advanced training school for many of these violent predators. I have seen numerous prison videos showing how they actively engage for hours in martial arts training with each other and practice techniques to disarm police officers during their endless free time in the general inmate population.

As a former U.S. Drug Enforcement Administration (DEA) firearms instructor, I have conducted officer survival training courses to many U.S. law enforcement personnel. During my tenure with the DEA office of international training, I have also conducted specialized training programs for foreign police officers in over 20 countries across the globe, and I know that the first question you are always asked during these training programs is if you have ever had to use deadly force yourself and shoot anyone. So I will get that question out of the way and respond, yes. When I was a rookie Dallas Police Officer, my first deadly force situation occurred back in 1979 when I shot a burglar. I have been forced to utilize deadly force on more than this one occasion during my 27- year law enforcement career. I want to emphasize however, just the fact that I have utilized deadly force in my career and survived is not what I believe makes me an excellent deadly force survival instructor, nor do I feel that is what qualifies me to relate these survival tips to you. Just because you have survived a deadly force encounter does not mean that you are good at teaching survival tactics.

Teaching is a skill that is totally different from your ability to perform as a police officer, soldier, or federal agent. Some of the best police and military instructors I ever worked with, or received training from, had never been forced to fire their firearm in the field during their entire career. In fact, even though the majority of police officers I know were involved in situations where they could have legally utilized deadly force, only a very small percentage of law enforcement personnel are actually forced to fire their weapons on the street during their career. This is because they had the common sense, wisdom, or training to utilize the basic survival rules outlined in this book.

The brilliant Chinese military historian Sun Tzu once stated, "The supreme art of war is to subdue the enemy without fighting." The fight you avoid, is the fight you always win, so don't voluntarily put yourself into a deadly force situation unless it is mandated to save your life, or that of a fellow law-abiding citizen. Depending on your distance from the adversary, escape by running away from the conflict to call for help might be a more prudent strategy, especially if you are outnumbered or outgunned (i.e. suspect has a shotgun and you only carry a small caliber pistol). As an armed citizen, your role is not to stop or apprehend criminals; that is what the police are for. One of the primary purposes of this book is to provide you with some common sense practical survival tips to hopefully prevent you from being put in a situation where you have to utilize deadly force in the first place, or if used, conduct yourself with poor tactics which result in your demise. Some of the most talented police officers and military personnel I ever worked with, were officers who were smart enough to plan operations and tactics in a manner so that the suspects or enemy personnel could be apprehended without the need for the utilization of deadly force. Most firearms instructors and gun magazine articles focus on issues such as the stopping power of the different calibers of weapons, how to have better accuracy, or what is the best type of holster or shooting positions to utilize. I cover those types of issues in this book, but the major focus of this book is the development of your tactics and the warrior mindset. You will hear me state many times in this survival manual that your mind is your greatest weapon.

I am probably the only deadly force survival instructor in the United States who has been employed by the DEA, CIA, FBI, and the Dallas Police Department. In over 27 years of my law enforcement career, (FBI Fingerprint Examiner 1977-1978, Dallas Police Officer 1978-1981, CIA Special Agent 1982-1985, and DEA Special Agent 1985-2006), I have made hundreds of arrests. I have attended numerous police and military training schools which include: DEA Firearms Instructor School, DEA Tactical Instructor School, DEA Defensive Tactics Instructor School, CIA Office of Security weapons training, FBI Instructor Development Course, Dallas Police Academy firearms training, U.S. Army Jungle Warfare school, U.S. Army ROTC officer basic training, and the U.S. Army Executive Protection course. I qualified to be awarded a membership in the "Possible Club". Only approximately 2% or less of the agents who graduate from the DEA and FBI Academy are given this distinction for accomplishing a perfect score on the federal combat firearms qualification course which has targets extending to 50 yards distance.

I want to note that one of the best firearms instruction courses I ever attended was conducted by an old cowboy named Dick Cook, a Sheriff's Deputy in Abilene, Kansas, who was a quick draw expert and master of instinct shooting from the hip. He had a range set up in the "Old Abilene Town" tourist attraction. Dick always literally shot from the hip without looking at his sights. Amazingly, he was quicker and many times more accurate at very close range as any United States Practical Shooting Association (U.S.P.S.A.) or Olympic shooter I have ever observed. In this book, I have constructed a short summary of the more noteworthy deadly force survival tactics rules that I learned from this broad variety of police and military training programs and instructors. I hope you never have to use these tactical guidelines, but if you do, they come from some of the best firearms and self-defense instructors in the world, and they could save your life.

Rule 1

Preparation & Safety

How quickly, and safely, can you access your firearm in an emergency? Gun owners who have small children in their home should consider the purchase of a gun vault, or at least utilize a combination lock briefcase to safely store loaded weapons. The author recommends a simple finger code release vault as shown above, or a simple combination lock briefcase in preference to locks that utilize keys. Biometric gun safes which only open with your fingerprint are also available, but expensive. Under the extreme stress of a home invasion or burglary, you do not want to be fumbling around looking for a key!

I know it is only common sense, but some of us don't have it. So remember that the first rule to survive a gunfight is to have a reliable and accurate gun already loaded and available if you need it. Will you have ready access to a reliable weapon when you need it? If your weapon and ammunition are separated and/or locked up in a safe, glove box, or trunk of your car, especially if it requires a key to access your storage location, you probably won't have time to obtain it before you are assaulted! Nonetheless, this creates a paradox; if you have small children in your home your paramount concern should be to make certain they do not have access to your firearms. A good practice is to have only one loaded pistol stored in a combination lock briefcase on a very high shelf in your bedroom closet. Let me tell you a short story about how even trained professionals are susceptible to human error and can sometimes make serious mistakes which could result in the death of a child.

Jim is a former highly decorated Dallas Police officer, as well as a very intelligent young man who went to law school, and later became an FBI Special Agent. Jim had always been very careful and prudent in the handling of firearms. One day, after working a 14-hour shift investigating a case for the FBI, Jim decided to stop by his friend John's home and watch a football game with him. John had a five-year-old son by the name of Matthew. While they were watching the football game, John went into the kitchen to make some sandwiches and Jim was left alone in the living room. Jim was extremely tired, exhausted from working his long shift, and started to relax. Lying on the couch in front of the television set, his holster and gun were becoming very uncomfortable on his hip, so he removed his holster and gun from his belt and placed them on top of the coffee table in front of him. He fell asleep within just a few minutes, leaving his holster and pistol unattended. When Jim woke up, he was shocked to see that John's five-year-old son, Matthew, was holding his pistol and looking down the barrel of the gun with his finger on the trigger! Jim immediately jumped up and took the pistol away from the small boy. Had Jim not awoken from his nap at that specific time, this story could have had a very tragic ending, not just for Matthew, but for Jim who would have certainly felt guilt-ridden the rest of his life.

I am a firm believer in the 2nd Amendment, but we must all realize that with freedom comes responsibility. If you decide to take advantage of your 2nd Amendment right to own or carry a firearm, you must also accept the responsibility to exercise extreme caution and safety when handling them. If you have children you should make certain to educate them on gun safety and keep firearms out of their reach until you are certain they are old enough to utilize them with proper safety.

The U.S. Center for Disease Control and Prevention reports from 2005-2010, almost 3,800 people in the U.S. died from unintentional shootings. More than a third of the victims were under 25 years of age. Millions of children live in homes with guns; however, it is estimated more than half of their parents do not keep their guns locked up. Guns should be kept locked up if you have small children, and storage keys and lock combinations should be hidden from children.

Most of the victims of unintentional shootings are boys. They are usually shot by a friend or relative, especially a brother. Half of all unintentional shooting deaths among children occur at home, and almost half occur in the home of a friend or relative. Most parents with guns think their children do not know where they hide them. However, one survey indicated 8 in 10 first graders know where their parents' guns are hidden. This is why I strongly recommend that if you must keep a loaded gun in a house with small children, keep the loaded pistol stored in a combination lock briefcase stored on a high shelf. In that manner, you still have fairly rapid access to it, as a combination lock is fairly quick and you don't have to search for a key, but it stays out of the reach of your children. Many gun owners think they are safe in just placing the loaded gun on a high shelf out of reach of children, without the combination lock briefcase. This is a serious error, as children are sometimes more clever than we think and have improvised talents we would not expect. Don't let your children see you put your gun away. I have seen videos from hidden cameras which show even very young children stacking boxes on top of each other so they could climb up to the top shelf in their parent's closet to grab and play with guns they saw their parents place there.

Now that I have pointed out the sad statistics about people accidentally killed by firearms, I'm sure that many gun control advocates reading this book are now screaming, "See, this is another good reason we should outlaw firearms!" Before you come to any decision on this topic, let me point out a few more statistics for your consideration:

- A dramatic spike in the number of Americans with permits to carry concealed weapons coincides with an equally stark drop in violent crime, according to a new study, which Second Amendment advocates say makes the case that more guns can mean safer streets. The study by the Crime Prevention Research Center found that 11.1 million Americans now have permits to carry concealed weapons, up from 4.5 million in 2007. The 146 percent increase has come even as both murder and violent crime rates have dropped by 22 percent.

- Law-abiding citizens use guns to defend themselves against criminals as many as 2.5 million times every year - or about 6,850 times a day. This means that each year, firearms are used 80 times more often to protect the lives of honest citizens than to take lives. As many as 200,000 women use a gun every year to defend themselves against sexual abuse (Kleck & Gertz, "Armed Resistance to Crime", at 185).
- There is the argument that more private gun ownership will lead to more accidents because the average citizen isn't sufficiently trained to use a weapon defensively. While gun accidents do occur, the Cato study indicates that they are the most overstated risks. Although every lost life is tragic, the proportion is not particularly startling in a population of over 300 million people.
- According to National Safety Council data, the total number of unintentional deaths from firearms sank to 554 in 2009, easily the lowest of any year back to 1903. In fact, it took from 1903 all the way until 1997 for the number of unintentional gunfire deaths to drop below 1,000. The all-time highs came in 1929 and 1930, when the number of such deaths reached 3,200 for two consecutive years. This decline is all the more striking considering the increase in population over this period. In 1904, there were 3.4 unintentional firearms deaths per 100,000 people. By 2009, that rate had fallen to 0.2 deaths per 100,000 people.
- Newsweek has reported that law-abiding American citizens using guns in self-defense during 2003 shot and killed two and one-half times as many criminals as police did, and with fewer than one-fifth as many incidents as police where an innocent person was mistakenly identified as a criminal (2% versus 11%).
- A Gallup poll in 2013, found that rural Americans are more than twice as likely to have a gun in the home as opposed to those living in large cities—yet urban areas have more gun violence than rural areas.
- In 2004, there were 3,308 unintentional drowning in the United States, an average of nine people per day. (Source: U.S. Center for Disease Control and Prevention 2006)
- In 2004, of all children 1-4 years old who died, 26% died

from drowning. Fatal drowning remains the second-leading cause of unintentional injury-related death for children ages 1 to 14 years. (Source: U.S. Center for Disease Control and Prevention 2005)
- 19% of drowning deaths involving children occur in public pools with certified lifeguards present. (Source: Drowning Prevention Foundation)
- A swimming pool is 14 times more likely than a motor vehicle to be involved in the death of a child age 4 and under. (Source: Orange County California Fire Authority)

I know some of you are shaking your head right now and wondering why I am providing statistics about drowning deaths in the U.S.? The reason is that the official statistics show it is obvious that swimming pools kill a significantly larger number of American children than do firearm accidents. The simple fact of the matter, is when it comes to accidents that kill children, statistics show the heart of the problem lies in water, cars, and fires. If the real agenda of gun control advocates is to save innocent lives, why don't they first lobby to eliminate swimming pools in the United States? It would certainly save a much larger number of people than gun control initiatives, especially since the U.S. cities with the highest homicide rates (Chicago, New Orleans, Detroit, and Washington D.C.) already have the strictest gun control laws in the U.S. which appear to have no effect on crime rates or shooting incidents.

If saving innocent lives is really the paramount concern, why is there no lobby to eliminate private swimming pools without lifeguards in the U.S.? In view of the documented statistics, how is a parent who doesn't watch his/her children around guns any more irresponsible than a parent who doesn't watch his/her children around a swimming pool? Well, you might argue that swimming pools are very important to provide recreation and pleasure to citizen's lives, but firearms also provide recreation and pleasure to many Americans via trap shooting, hunting, target shooting, and competitive shooting events. In addition, they have a practical utilization, far more important than swimming pools, in that they save thousands of law abiding citizens from becoming the victims of crimes every year and thereby also save many innocent lives. Remember the following rules of gun safety and train your children that if they see a gun, they should do four things:

- **Stop**
- **Don't touch it**
- **Leave the area**
- **Call an adult**

Seven Primary Rules of Gun Safety

1. Don't have loaded guns unsecured or near young children
2. Get training—enough to be proficient with your weapon
3. Never mix guns with drugs or alcohol
4. Always assume all guns are always loaded
5. Never point a gun at anything you don't want to destroy
6. Always keep your finger off the trigger until your sights are on the target and you are ready to shoot
7. Know your target and what is beyond it

Rule 2

The Warrior Mindset

The "Warrior Mindset" is to be able to recognize a threat and respond appropriately, which is just as important as your accuracy with a firearm. Remember that your mind is your most valuable and powerful weapon! The proper mindset is essential to keep your mind from freezing up during the stress of an attack. You must be mentally prepared to take decisive action immediately in response to a deadly threat. One of the best officer survival instructors I was ever trained by was a DEA Special Agent by the name of Frank White. The charismatic Frank White, who when asked during a trial why he'd shot a notorious Florida drug-dealer nine times, responded: "Nine? Because I ran out of bullets." Frank White became a legend in the DEA as he was involved in more police shootings than any agent in DEA history. He reportedly placed a total of over 30 rounds into the bodies of drug traffickers during his DEA career.

Many in law enforcement first learn firearms and deadly force tactics in the military. After discharge, most put those skills behind them. However, men like Frank White who came to DEA after service in Vietnam, chose to transfer not only his deadly force skills but the will to use them in the domestic war front. The younger DEA Special Agents he later trained knew him as one of the "Jurassic Narcs"... a fitting description for this elite endangered species.

Most of the Jurassic Narcs came to law enforcement after a tour in Vietnam, where they'd witnessed not only the stunning defeat inflicted on the United States but had watched helplessly as heroin, LSD and marijuana attacked the moral fiber of the military. The images fixed in their memories of comrades transformed into drug zombies, together with friends dead from overdoses, prompted hundreds of veterans to enlist in the war on drugs. They joined Lyndon Johnson's Bureau of Narcotics and Dangerous Drugs and later Richard Nixon's replacement agency, the Drug Enforcement Administration, or DEA.

"You can teach a student to shoot under adversity, but not the will to fight through it."
–Police Instructor Frank White

Frank survived numerous firefights in Vietnam where he was awarded the Silver Star and numerous other military decorations. During his time in Vietnam, and thereafter in law enforcement, Frank would be known for his decisiveness under fire. Decisive action is the key to survival on the battlefield. Frank White would later advise me that it is also the key to survival in law enforcement, but in law enforcement you are operating with a distinct disadvantage to the military battlefield environment. In law enforcement situations you must always be on guard, as you do not usually know the identity of the threat in advance. The enemy is not wearing a uniform and our legal system mandates you can only use deadly force in response to a threat to your life or to save the life of an innocent citizen. Unfortunately, action is usually quicker than reaction, therefore the criminal has a distinct advantage over the law enforcement officer or an armed civilian in that only the criminal can decide when, and if, he will initiate an attack which requires a deadly force response. Vigilance and the "Warrior Mindset" mental preparation is the key to officer and armed civilian survival. The well prepared law enforcement officer's mind is always racing in anticipation of how to respond in a myriad of potential deadly situations, knowing he who hesitates could very well be lost.

Frank White became renowned as the father of DEA tactical training and I am sure his training has saved the lives of more than one DEA special agent. Some of his best advice; don't take a seat in a restaurant without your back to the wall, look before you enter any building or area, maintain ready access to your sidearm, take corners wide and use the quick-peek technique. Don't just run into the middle of a room with your gun drawn, and be alert for hiding places where you could be ambushed. Always remember to look for the red flags that signal a suspect is carrying a concealed weapon. Suspects who are covertly armed often glance nervously at where their gun is carried, or touch it on their side for reassurance that it's still there. Proper firearms' training, to prepare for attack, is essential to survival. The issue that some police officers, and even much fewer armed citizens understand, is the extreme effects of stress and adrenaline to the unprepared mind. In those first few seconds of an attack, your parasympathetic nervous system (fight or flight) will take over control from your mind, causing you to freeze, run, or respond with the muscle memory of how you trained.

The mechanics of shooting a firearm are relatively simple. The techniques to obtain a proper sight picture, weapon grip, shooting platform, etc. will be discussed further in RULE 8 (Firearms Shooting Fundamentals). Frank White's excellence in training is the psychology of the mental preparation in knowing the proper preset of your heart and mind. This stuff is nothing new. This knowledge is thousands of years old and you see it used in martial arts training schools across the world. Its principals are based on discipline, preparation and awareness, as well as tactics. These black belts and martial arts experts are killers, but they are killers who don't need to kill to achieve victory. If you are a soldier, police officer, or even an armed citizen with a concealed carry permit, you had better be mentally prepared to kill, if the circumstances mandate deadly force. If you are not prepared to use this deadly force you should not carry that firearm and should probably carry a non-lethal TASER® weapon instead. It's the same mindset as the Ninja, the Samurai, the Roman Centurion, or the Greek Spartan warrior. It has always been the same, but some people just don't get it.

Louis Awerbuck is another self-defense instructor with a similar quality of training as Frank White. Louis used this explanation as to why some people "just don't get it": "Some of the people who don't get it are highly professional, skilled people — like a commercial pilot, a neurosurgeon, somebody who cannot afford to make the slightest slip in his occupation, so he overthinks every single thing when he's firing a weapon. They'll 'what if' things to death. Other people who don't get it are not really fighting-oriented. From what I've seen, I think it's a societal thing. Let's face it, in North America you can pretty much buy anything you want. So people tend to think that if you pay a certain amount of money to be taught how to do something with a firearm, the net result at the end of the day is that you will be able to do it. It's like paying to have your brakes fixed, or paying for an appendectomy. They are paying for a service and they expect it to be done. They don't figure they need any ability themselves or that they're going to have to put some of themselves into it."

Awerbuck described what the non-warriors do when they get in trouble: "They will probably have their pistol taken away, because really and truly deep down inside, they know they are not prepared to take life even in defense of their own. So they'll probably have their pistol taken away, get shot with their own pistol, and then the crook will leave with their pistol and shoot another person with it." Many self-defense instructors have agreed that one of their primary concerns is that a significant number of the civilians they train are not capable of shooting someone. Awerbuck continued, "Not looking into their faces, looking into their eyes from six feet away and doing it. A lot of people will go out and shoot Bambi in the Coconino Forest and not think twice about it but couldn't bring themselves to do it to a human, who just happens to be an animal walking on his back legs. If I'm afraid of you, in fear of my life, I need to do something about it."

"We've grown up in a society where other people protect us. We expect to make a phone call and somebody will be there. It's like pulling the blanket over your head to protect yourself from the bogey man. It's all a mind deal. Everybody keeps saying the gun is just a tool. It's a piece of metal. How many times are you going to let a two-pound piece of metal and plastic outwit you? We're not talking about flying a Tomcat here, this is not brain surgery. But it is psychology."

"Because the gun still represents the equality of power. Whether it's a little old lady from Pasadena or a muscle man, with a gun they can deliver equal power from a distance, whether six feet or sixty yards. Some people are realizing the glory days are gone. The world is pretty much hell-bent for destruction, because we're in for a worldwide religious war from hell, this is going to make the other world wars look like Sunday picnics. Right now you have laws. You can't carry a gun here, you can't do this there, you can't spit on the sidewalk, these may be fine in a peaceful society. But when you've got a society that's gone mad, worldwide, the law of the jungle supersedes all other laws."

Frank White always advised us to "Live in Condition YELLOW" and be vigilant for your survival! What did Frank mean when he stated we should live in condition YELLOW for survival? These color codes have to do with common sense situational awareness, not paranoia or hyper-vigilance. When you first wake up in the morning, you are in condition WHITE. You are totally relaxed and probably unaware of your surroundings, so you are unprepared to swiftly react to any threats. This is why prudent law enforcement officers prefer to conduct raids on homes in the middle of the night, or very early in the morning, when the suspects are asleep or in condition WHITE. This makes them less likely to react quickly and obtain weapons or have the motivation to resist arrest. With drug addicts, this can be a little tricky to ascertain when they are sleeping, take for example a methamphetamine addict who may stay awake three days straight while on a drug binge.

Condition YELLOW is higher up on the color scale. In condition YELLOW you probably have already had your first cup of coffee. You are now very aware of your environment, but in a relaxed state of alertness. The next stage, condition ORANGE, is a more heightened awareness where your senses have given you reason to suspect a particular danger is present. I have observed that some police officers seem to have a 6th sense to detect danger, which is sometimes difficult to define in court testimony. Many police officers with this 6th sense can walk into a bar and have an immediate intuition about a suspect that involves more than just eye contact and body language. You cannot define it. Some criminals just have an aura of evil when you are in their presence. When you sense this danger, your system gears up and you go into condition ORANGE. This stimulation is also known as the fight or flight syndrome. In condition ORANGE your blood pressure increases and your adrenaline starts to flow as you suspect danger. This evolved response has developed so we could fight better or run faster when we encounter danger. The next step up the ladder is condition RED. Condition RED is when you actually begin to fight or flight and your heart is pounding and adrenaline flowing at the maximum.

It is important to maintain condition YELLOW, so you are aware of your environment to detect danger. This allows your system to transition easily for the jump up to condition RED, responding with more strength and speed. To put this in simple terms, if you are already going 30 mph in your car, you can punch the accelerator and get up to full speed quicker than if you haven't even started your engine. We are most vulnerable when we are in condition WHITE, the most common condition people maintain most of the day. Many people walk around in condition WHITE and fall victim to environmental blindness. They are absorbed in their own thoughts and not aware of what is going on around them and this can be especially dangerous if you are a police officer. People in condition WHITE simply don't see or hear the attacker coming in time to do anything about it to escape or avoid the attack.

Some defensive tactics instructors also believe that you are more likely to survive a gunshot wound if you were in condition RED, than if you were in condition WHITE, when you are shot. It is believed that when you are in condition RED you are fully alert, stimulated, and most of your blood has rushed to your vital organs such as the heart and lungs. Humans have developed this response so that if a tiger bit your hand off while in condition RED, more of your blood has already rushed to the vital organs (white knuckle syndrome) and you are a little less likely to bleed to death, or at least it will take longer to do so. They also speculate you are more likely to go into shock if you are shot while in condition WHITE.

Condition YELLOW causes your peripheral vision to be in high gear, allowing you to see any and all approaching danger. Your heightened awareness will alert you to an attack that is coming and triggers you to be prepared to fight or run. Alertness to this danger can make the difference of whether or not you are a survivor, or a crime statistic. Beware of distractions. The use of seductively clad females is a form of distraction commonly utilized. Also, be careful to avoid the frequent mistake of accidentally exposing your weapon when in a concealed carry status. Remember, the outline of your gun appears when pushed against your clothing. We all make mistakes and get complacent. We forget to check to see if the "imprint" of our weapon, and/or holster, is exposed, thereby alerting the public, and the bad guys, that you are in a concealed carry status.

Situational awareness is simply knowing what's going on around you, all the time. It sounds easy in principle, but in reality requires much practice. It is taught to soldiers and police officers, but it is also an important skill for armed civilians to learn as well. In a dangerous situation, being aware of a threat, seconds before everyone else, can keep you and your loved ones safe. Self Defense instructor John Duncan defines awareness as follows, "Awareness is our ability to remain oriented in the world. For self- preservation, we need to have various kinds of awareness: Strategic, Situational, Tactical, and Combat. Strategic awareness is knowing the "lay of the land", where danger usually lies, that it is not a good idea to go to a dark isolated ATM in a bad part of town at 2 AM. It is a guidepost for staying alive; we should know where danger typically resides. Situational awareness is knowing what is going on around you—all the time. Tactical awareness has to do with an emerging danger. What are my options for escape? Avoidance? Survival? Where are my nearest weapons? Combat awareness is having your mind in survival mode during an actual attack and fight. All of these kinds of awareness integrate with each other to keep us safe. They are not "paranoia" or "fear". Instead, they are the mind of a warrior as it manifests itself in each moment." Be aware, stay alive, be a warrior!

Self-defense also involves being in good physical condition. I am not saying you need to be a marathon runner, or a black belt in karate, but you should be able to walk at least a couple miles without being exhausted, or you might have a really hard time maintaining control of your handgun if your assailant tries to take it away from you. In close quarters, your ability to fight with your gun is just as important as being an exceptional shooter. Don't assume that strapping on a gun precludes you from having to defend yourself empty-handed.

The type of threat you're facing may not justify drawing your weapon in the first place. For instance, drawing your gun in response to an aggressive drunk in a bar who starts shoving you around, will probably not be considered a reasonable response. However, if he is much larger than you are and is beating you unconscious, or pulls out a broken beer bottle or other weapon, most reasonable jurors would consider that as legal justification for drawing your weapon. This is why it is so important that you make certain you have a solid grasp of all the self-defense laws in your state before you even consider carrying a concealed weapon. The more familiar you are with laws pertaining to the use of force, up to and including deadly force in self-defense, the less likely you'll be to hesitate when you need to act. Remember that from a legal perspective, your actions will be judged on their "reasonableness" based on the totality of the circumstances. This is another reason I state that your mind is your greatest weapon. Know the law and maintain a "Warrior Mindset", if you are going to take on the huge responsibility of obtaining a Concealed Carry Permit (CCP).

Rule 3

Take Advantage Of Cover, If It Is Available

Remember to always take advantage of cover when you draw your weapon. It will be a great deal more difficult for your adversary to hit you with a bullet, if the only target area exposed is your gun hand and dominant eyeball for sight picture. Anyone who has ever served in the infantry knows the importance of cover and concealment tactics. They don't have you dig foxholes for the fun of it. Cover is anything that you can get behind to potentially stop bullets (trees, walls, foxholes, car doors, etc.). Concealment is anything which prevents you from being seen by the enemy, but does not stop bullets. Tall grass and bushes may hide you from the enemy, but will not stop bullets from hitting you.

Those who have served in the military are fully aware of the huge advantage of firing rounds from behind cover, but most armed civilians probably don't even think about this when they get into a gunfight. Remember when you practice shooting, to also practice shooting from behind cover. Under stress, you will revert to your training. Train yourself to attempt to always take cover before you shoot. Just as soldiers have trained themselves to always take cover when they hear incoming artillery rounds, you should try to train yourself to take cover in a gunfight scenario. You should also practice, at least on a few occasions, shooting with your weak hand, in the event you are ever shot in your strong hand or forearm during a gunfight and need to transition to your weak hand.

Many police trainers also teach students to shoot their firearms while moving, with the idea that you are less likely to be struck by incoming fire if you are a moving target. In addition to shooting while moving, almost all police trainers advocate moving to cover, if cover is available. The logic of this is simple. Making yourself a moving target and seeking bullet-resistant cover can only help your chances of winning a gunfight. The old romantic image of two gunfighters squaring off in the middle of the street from Hollywood westerns was rarely accurate. The actors were always shown bravely facing each other but in reality, opponents were more often scampering for cover. They were frequently drinking, missing ordinarily easy shots, and sometimes continue to shoot until their pistols were empty. In reality, there is usually much more involved in winning a gunfight than a simple "Old West" quick draw match where he who un-holsters first, wins.

There is no such thing as a fair gunfight. There is dead and there is alive, fair has nothing to do with it!

Examples of the Utilization of Cover During Training Programs

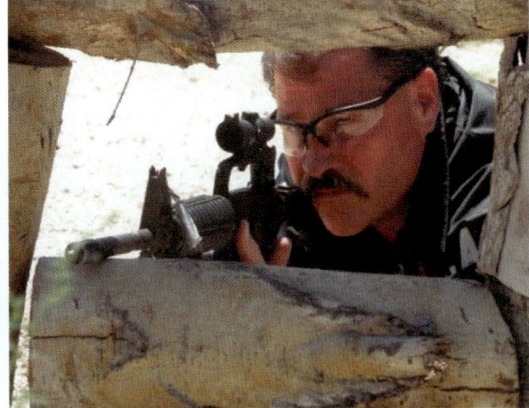

Practice shooting from behind cover during your firearms training.

Take proper cover during felony arrest traffic stops. Observe the small amount of target area exposed.

10 Keys to Prevent an Ambush in Your Car

In view of the recent assassination of two NYPD officers while they were sitting in their police car, Major Travis Yates of the Tulsa Police Department has provided the following suggested tactical guidelines to help prevent these type of ambush attacks on police in the future. While rare, ambush attacks in patrol vehicles do occur and the confinement of a vehicle can make it difficult to prepare for. Here are ten things to keep in mind to mitigate the risk of ambush in your patrol vehicle.

1. Paperwork should be done in a secured location where citizens cannot approach your car.
2. You should always know an escape plan. Park for a rapid exit and leave a cushion with cars around you on the road.
3. Check mirrors often and observe those around you.
4. Make sure you aren't being followed. A few left turns will help you identify potential danger.
5. Try to avoid using the same routes daily. This vigilance should continue while driving home.

6. Scan parking lots and intersections as you enter them.
7. Make eye contact with others when you can. Pay particular attention to those that avoid looking at you.
8. Use caution when cars stop suddenly in front of you, or when they fail to pull completely off the road when they stop.
9. When suspects exit their vehicle, if they leave their door open, that could be an indication they plan on attacking and running back to their car.
10. Never let someone approach you while you are sitting in your car—get out of the vehicle and be prepared to take cover!

A Police Officer in Durham, North Carolina, utilized a couple of these tactics in December 2014 and it probably saved his life. Officer J. T. West was on high alert because of the recent murder of the two NYPD officers in New York. While sitting in a parked car, he spotted the approach of two men in his squad car's rear-view mirror. Officer West immediately exited his vehicle to confront the pair, then one of the would-be assassins opened fire on West without saying a word. West dove for cover while the gunman fired six shots at him. All six shots missed West (probably because he dived for cover), but one round did hit the patrol car. West fired two rounds of return fire, but it wasn't known if West wounded either of the men.

West injured his wrist when he dove for cover behind a staircase at a nearby vacant apartment building. He was treated at a nearby hospital and released. Police said West and the men, who ran from the scene, never exchanged words. This attempted assassination mimicked the tactics used to murder NYPD officers Rafael Ramos and Wenjian Liu on December 20, 2014. The Baltimore gang member who killed those two NYPD officers walked up on the right rear of the officers' marked police car and opened fire without warning. The gang member in that instance — who committed suicide minutes later in a subway as authorities closed in — cited the deaths of Michael Brown and Eric Garner by police as his excuse to "put pigs in a blanket."

Suggested Tactics for the Armed Citizen

If you are the armed citizen who is being followed by a suspicious vehicle, I advise you to take the following advice. Take four or five turns in your vehicle off the main routes of transit in your city. If you are still being followed, just pull over and look in your rear view mirror. If the suspicious vehicle pulls in behind you, you have confirmed something suspicious is taking place. Do not turn off your engine or step outside your vehicle to confront the occupants, but call the police and advise you are being followed by a suspicious vehicle and wait for them to arrive at the location. Make sure you give the police a detailed description of both yourself, and the suspects, so they are not confused about who are the bad guys when they arrive at the location. If you do not recognize the occupants of the suspicious vehicle, and they get out of their vehicle and approach you, drive off immediately and drive to the nearest police station before they can run up to the side of your vehicle for an assault, trapping you in your vehicle.

If you encounter an incident of "Road Rage", do not pull over and DO NOT get out of your vehicle. Cars can kill you just as easily as a firearm. Road rage and aggressive driving claim thousands of lives every year. Take road rage seriously, remember you could be dealing with an unstable individual with a gun, or a person who may ram your car or attack you. Treat every road rage situation as a potentially dangerous one. Psychologists recommend that you try to get away from the conflict as soon as possible. I know it is sometimes very difficult to not respond to these jerks, but DO NOT make faces or gestures, yell, flash your lights, or honk your horn. You need to watch the individual to make certain he does not draw a weapon, but try not to make eye contact to further aggravate him.

Know your role as an armed citizen. Carrying a gun doesn't obligate you to take action, even when you are a witness to a crime that would justify a deadly force response. It is not your job to apprehend criminals. That is what the police are for. If you want to be a hero, you should find the nearest recruiting station for the military or local law enforcement. Carrying a handgun is something that should primarily be conducted for the personal safety of yourself and your family. It should be viewed as a mundane, boring task to buckle on your holster every morning, like buckling your seatbelt. There is no guarantee that drawing your gun will save the day. In fact, you could unintentionally make things much worse.

You never know if the bad guy has unidentified partners who could shoot you in the back if you draw down on him (See case example in RULE 18). Even if the bad guy is working alone, your response could prompt a shootout that might not otherwise have occurred. You should only take action, and draw your weapon, if the criminal has made clear his intent to injure or kill you, or harm other innocent parties. Remember there are no absolutes, and your best course of action might be to run, to call the police, or simply be a good witness when the police arrive.

Rule 4

The Triangle Of Gunfight Survival

```
              WARRIOR MINDSET
                    ▲
                   / \
                  /   \
                 /     \
                /       \
               /         \
              /           \
             /             \
            /_____\
   TACTICS                   MARKSMANSHIP
```

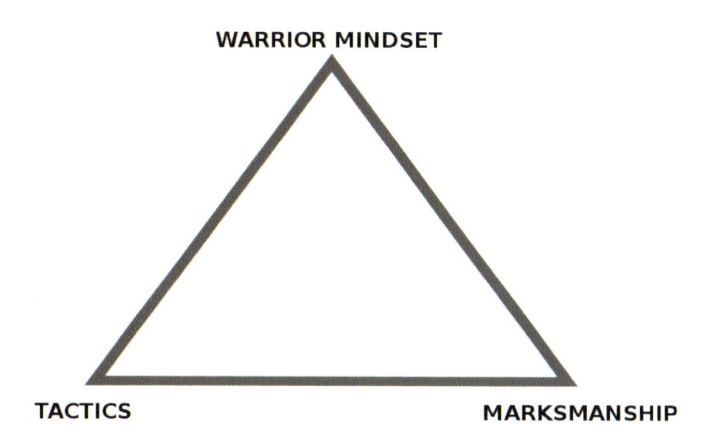

    The triangle of gunfight survival is a mixture of the survival warrior mindset, movement for cover and tactics, and firearm marksmanship accuracy. Most armed citizens have the mistaken impression that a high caliber handgun and good marksmanship are the only skills needed to win a gunfight. Being a fast draw and an accurate shooter are very important, but if you don't have the warrior mindset to shoot without hesitation you might still lose the battle, even though you are a better shot than your adversary. Those who have actually been in deadly force encounters will tell you that most people will hesitate before taking a life, that split second or seconds of hesitation can make a big difference. It can give your opponent time to take the first shot, or to take cover which will give him a distinct advantage. Expertise in the mixture of warrior mindset, proper tactics to take a position of advantage (cover, back up, superior weapons, sun in your opponents eyes, sobriety, tritium night sights on your pistol, wearing a bullet proof vest, utilization of a ballistic shield, flashlight, etc.), combined with firearms marksmanship are more important than skilled shooting alone. An example of one of the tactics that will help you survive a deadly force encounter is to obtain the right equipment and training to prepare yourself for a shootout in the dark and low light situations.

Prepare for a Gunfight in Low Light Conditions

Most deadly force incidents take place in low light conditions, so I recommend you obtain night sights for your pistol and also practice shooting your pistol with a flashlight. My first deadly force incident involved shooting a burglar at a distance of approximately 20 yards in a dark hallway. I know I would never have hit him at that distance in the dark, but for the fact that I had the tactical advantage of tritium night sights on my pistol. I wouldn't have been able to see my sights without this equipment advantage. These night sights are set up so that the light on the sights can only be seen from behind the pistol; therefore, you have the advantage of not revealing your position in the dark to your adversary. They come in different models and most cost less than $200.

One of the most obvious prerequisites of shooting is that one has to see the target, in relation to his or her sight, before they can hit it. A standard three dot tritium night sight, or the slightly larger reflex sight, greatly mitigates the challenges attendant to low-light shooting. While only an artificial light source, such as a flashlight or a spotlight, can provide the illumination needed for target identification, the three colored dots on the Trijicon HD tritium night sight and the single "colored dot" in a reflex sight greatly enhance any shooter's ability to see the sight in relation to the target. The evolution of engineering, LED and battery technology has made the use of reflex red-dot sights on handguns not only feasible but practical in terms of size, reliability and effectiveness. While no gun can overcome poor shooting fundamentals, these type of night sights will improve a good shooter's effectiveness.

Trijicon HD™ Night Sights

These sights have a brilliant aiming point that's only enhanced by its unique high-visibility color configurations. Add the advanced and feature-packed body design and they are certain to shine — even in the most demanding of situations. With superior aiming point visibility, faster sight acquisition and features designed to enhance usability in emergency situations these sights are the most advanced in the world — and the clear choice for the demanding needs of law enforcement.

Trijicon RMR®

The Trijicon RMR (Ruggedized Miniature Reflex) sight is one of the most rugged miniature red dot sights available. It is made from 7075-T6 aluminum to MIL-spec standards and has a patented shape that absorbs impacts and diverts stresses away from the lens, increasing durability. Available in LED, Adjustable LED, or Dual Illuminated versions, and with dot sizes ranging from 3.25 MOA to 13 MOA you are sure to find what fits your needs. The RMR is a versatile sight that illuminates in any lighting condition.

Rifle and Shotgun Low Light Sights

In the dark it is very important to be able to see your sights when a dangerous animal, or human predator, attacks you!

Trijicon ACOG

The Trijicon ACOG (Advanced Combat Optical Gunsight) is a fixed power, compact riflescope with an illuminated reticle pattern for use in bright to low/no light. The ACOG sight is designed to be extremely durable and reliable. Combining traditional, precise distance marksmanship with CQB speed, many variants include a bullet drop compensated (BDC) reticle. Every feature of its design was chosen for a single purpose: to provide increased hit potential in all lighting conditions.

Shooting With A Flashlight

Both of these styles of shooting with a flashlight have advantages and disadvantages. The technique displayed above may allow better accuracy as you have both hands supporting your firearm. However, it has the disadvantage in that if the suspect shoots for the light, you are directly behind it and he will therefore be more likely to hit you. The technique displayed below has the advantage of a greater chance the suspect will miss you, if he cannot get a sight picture on your body because he is blinded by the flashlight, and he therefore shoots directly at the light.

Photo Courtesy of DPD Tactical Officer Marshall Milligan

We have all experienced the fear of hearing a loud noise wake you up from a comfortable night's sleep. Sometimes we hear a loud noise that makes us fear that someone may be breaking into your house. When you hear that ubiquitous bump in the night, what is your first move? When you jump out of bed and start fumbling around the house in the dark you don't want to have to search for both a flashlight and a gun at the same time. In situations where you don't want to turn on the lights, don't have lights available in that area, or can't illuminate the entire area, having a flashlight is a must. You have seen the television shows with the police holding a flashlight in one hand and the gun in the other. Sometimes with their wrists crossed for stability. Why hassle with this? Having a gun-mounted flashlight for your pistol, rifle, or shotgun is a more simple, tactically sound, and safer solution.

Firearms with attached flashlight are the most practical selection for low light shooting situations!

Are Warning Shots A Good Idea?

I never say never, as there are some very unusual exceptions to almost every general rule (i.e., you are in an extremely remote area of the Nevada desert and you can see that no one aside from you and your attacker is within three miles of your location), but I would strongly advise you, <u>DO NOT fire warning shots!</u> Verbal threats that you will shoot if your adversary does not stop moving toward you or refuses to drop his weapon are good, but firing warning shots is almost always a very bad idea. Remember that you are responsible for every bullet that leaves your firearm and if you shoot up into the air you have no idea where that bullet will land or if it might ricochet and hit something, even an innocent person, you never intended to shoot. How do you explain to the police and the prosecutor that you felt you were in grave danger, truly in fear of your life, if you didn't feel you needed to shoot your assailant to stop him?

Rule 5

Target Acquisition

Knowing where and how to shoot a violent criminal to stop an attack is very important. The caliber and magazine capacity of your weapon is not as important as the reliability and easy access of your weapon, as well as your marksmanship capabilities with it. You notice that I stated "stop an attack", not "kill the suspect". Your goal should be to stop the threat posed to you, not to kill the suspect. Unfortunately, you will sometimes be forced to kill the suspect to stop the attack and save your own life. The goal of police and the armed citizen should be to stop a threat during a deadly force encounter as quickly as possible. You do not shoot to kill, you shoot to stay alive. Whether or not a death occurs is of no consequence, as long as the threat of death or serious injury to the law enforcement officer or armed citizen and innocent third parties is eliminated. You are morally entitled to save your own life and innocent third parties from a violent assault!

Most self-defense instructors will advise you to take two quick shots to the center of mass of your adversary (known as a double tap), then make a quick evaluation, and take aim for a well-placed shot to the center of the head if your adversary is still threatening. Real gunfights are not like what you see in many movies, with the exception of a few very realistic gunfights, such as the one shown in the movie *Taxi Driver*. It is noted that a medical doctor once told me you can shoot someone directly in the heart with a .357 magnum and they can still live up to 45 seconds. Take a look at your watch and you will see that is a lot of time for your adversary to return fire, so don't forget that rule in the previous rule about taking cover. If you've watched many old Hollywood westerns, you would think that all you have to do is shoot your adversary once and they drop like a log, but in the real world this is not usually the case. There have been numerous cases where police officers have shot suspects multiple times and the suspects still lived long enough to return fire and kill a police officer.

Sometimes the suspect only had a knife, but still lived long enough to run at the police officer, thrust his knife into him and kill him, even though the suspect was shot multiple times in the chest (see RULE

17: "21-Foot Rule"). There are two ways in which bullets incapacitate your adversary. The first being from massive hemorrhaging (blood loss) and the physical and psychological state of your adversary (a suspect pumped up on drugs may feel less pain). The second way to incapacitate your adversary is to shut down the central nervous system, the only way to instantly turn his lights out.

The only way to be certain you will take out your attacker immediately (which is what a police sniper would need to do if the suspect was holding a gun to the head of a hostage), is to shoot the suspect in the triangle of death, that upside down triangle area of the face which covers the eyes and nose (see photo illustration below). Frank White used to say that shooting someone in the chest is aiming for the "hydraulics" which may kill them, but it could take time which could cost you your life. In some cases, the only way to take out a violent criminal immediately, who is still threatening you after a double tap to the chest, is to shoot them between the eyes, the CNS "electronics" which will shut them down immediately. Ironically, this is the same tactic that you see the cast members of the fictional TV show "The Walking Dead" utilize to take out zombies. Sometimes violent criminals under the influence of drugs can be almost as difficult to stop as one of those TV zombies. Exercise extreme caution with violent criminals under the influence of drugs and the mentally ill. Suspects under the influence of powerful drugs like phencyclidine (PCP) and methamphetamine are sometimes extremely insensitive to pain and may require several well placed shots to stop the threat. This is a gruesome subject that is difficult for an individual with morals and any sensitivity to human suffering to talk about, but if you get involved in a gunfight it could save your life.

Target Selection

Triangle of Probable Death & Immediate Incapacitation

First Fire A Double Tap to Center of Mass of Target

When taking down an attacker be sure to fire two shots to the chest region, followed by one or two to the triangle of death region, if the first two shots did not incapacitate the suspect.

Rule 6

Stress And The Unarmed Suspect Can Be A Killer

Stress experienced by police officers and military veterans creates significant health risks and can lead to post traumatic stress disorder or alcohol abuse problems. Police officers also have a high rate of suicide in this nation, possibly the highest. They have a high divorce rate, about second in the nation. They are problem drinkers about twice as often as the general population. These facts are warning signals for unseen problems that are not being handled. Researchers use suicide, divorce and alcoholism rates as three key indexes of stress in a group of people. In a previous rule, I spoke about the color codes of how the stress of a violent assault can affect your adrenaline and heart rate, but in this rule we are also going to discuss how the daily stress of life in general (divorce, death, illness, substance abuse, domestic abuse, child abuse, etc.) can be a very negative factor for your physical and psychological health. These are issues frequently encountered by police in daily calls for assistance.

Most people are not aware of the extreme physical effects that stress and adrenaline have on the mind and body during a violent attack. The stress during a life and death gunfight or physical assault can also destroy your firearms accuracy if you are not mentally prepared. It should be noted that police officers miss between 70 and 80% of their shots during actual shooting incidents on the street, but perform far better on non-stress target shooting qualifications.

It is obvious that stress will dramatically affect your shooting performance. You need to develop muscle memory that makes shooting your firearm an instinctive reaction via extensive training. If you have to think about it, you might hesitate, and hesitation means possible freezing or poor shooting under stress. If your mind is in condition WHITE (see Rule 2: Warrior Mind Set) you have environmental blindness. If you are preoccupied, you may be absorbed in your own thoughts in condition WHITE and not aware of what is going on around you. This may cause you to simply not see or hear the attacker coming in time to escape the attack. The only time it is really good to be in condition WHITE, is when you are asleep or engaged in meditation. Moderate amounts of sleep, or this type of escape from reality via meditation, are good for your physical health as your body and mind heals in condition WHITE, but it is very dangerous for a police officer, medical doctor, pilot, or construction worker to be in condition WHITE when they are working, or even your average citizen to be in condition WHITE when they are driving a car.

People react to stress in different ways. If you are under heavy stress, you might be experiencing the opposite extreme from condition WHITE and find you are semi-paranoid, frequently in condition ORANGE or RED, even though you have no real threat in your environment, your mind and parasympathetic nervous system cannot slow down from the memory of a previous terrifying encounter. The parasympathetic system is responsible for the body's ability to recuperate and return to a balanced state (known as "homeostasis") after experiencing pain or stress. The sympathetic system is also known as the "fight or flight" response. If you are on this opposite extreme of frequent condition ORANGE or RED from stress without a real danger present, it might actually improve your ability to survive a deadly force encounter, but is extremely bad for your physical health. Our bodies are designed to return to a state of homeostasis, a balance of highs and lows, for your long-term health. If you are always driving your car at 120 mph, the engine is more likely to quit sooner than a prudent driver's car.

Chronic stress numbs people's sensitivity. They can't stand to continually see human misery. They must sometimes stop feeling and put on the police mask to survive emotionally. People wear different types of masks, depending on their profession. Salesmen always have the mask of being happy, friendly, cordial, and caring to create a bond with the customer and help close a sale. Police usually keep their emotions hidden to display objectivity and professionalism. The police mask is to always display strength and no emotion, except possibly aggressive emotion to display extreme strength. Remember the famous line of police Sergeant Joe Friday in the Dragnet TV series, "Just the facts ma'am, just give me the facts!" It is not that they don't care, but rather a psychological defense mechanism that they use to protect them from emotional suffering they see every day. The police and soldier's minds have this defense mechanism so they can continue working in horrible situations. If police and soldiers felt the normal sensitivity of the general public they might fall apart, and if they show too much emotion it can be viewed as weakness on the battlefield or in police street survival situations. As they become less sensitive to the suffering of others, they can become insensitive to their own suffering. We are all aware that stress is part of the police profession and working conditions. In the past, police management did not recognize stress as a problem affecting their officers. There is now significant evidence and research showing that unmanaged stress can lead to anxiety, depression, and post-traumatic stress disorder (PTSD). Police officers consistently encounter stressors in receiving call after call, which saps their strength. Debilitation from this daily stress accumulates, thus making officers more vulnerable to traumatic incidents and normal pressures of life. The weakening process is often too slow to see; neither a person nor his friends are aware of the damage being done.

The stress of potential negative public media coverage can be a factor in a police officer's stress level and possible failure to respond adequately in some situations. If a medical doctor screws up during a surgery, the cost of his malpractice insurance might go up, but he will rarely lose his medical license unless there are several repeated errors in the future; whereas, if a police officer makes a serious error and shoots the wrong person, or accidentally hits an innocent bystander, in a deadly force situation, he will probably lose his job and may even face criminal charges. Veteran police officer and firearms expert Bryan de Klerk states, "How many times have you heard anti-police community groups proclaim, 'He wasn't armed. The police had no right to shoot him!' If a police officer or armed citizen walks up to someone out of the blue and shoots them dead in the street, that's a totally different story, and this type of individual should be prosecuted to the full extent of the law, but shooting an unarmed assailant during a life-threatening fight in the street is another. The police officer who is physically assaulted, and feels he may soon be unconscious, does not know the intentions of the attacker and cannot allow himself to be overpowered, lest he become one of that 10% of the police officers who are killed with their own weapon. You also have no idea if your attacker is armed with a hidden weapon, but they just haven't pulled it out yet. You cannot wait until you are unable to defend yourself to find out."

The practical solution to help lower the number of police having to shoot an unarmed assailant, who physically attacks them, is to issue all police officers the non-lethal TASER® conducted electrical weapon. The real tragedy of the recent police shooting in Ferguson, Missouri, is that Officer Wilson did not have the opportunity to utilize a TASER. This could have possibly allowed him to exercise the alternate option of shooting the non-lethal TASER to stop the attack which put him in fear for his life. It is unknown if Officer Wilson was ever issued a TASER, and it may not have mattered since Michael Brown reportedly escalated the threat to Wilson by attempting to wrestle Officer Wilson's gun away from him in the squad car at the very onset of this conflict. It would probably cost the U.S. taxpayer less to issue a TASER to every police officer in this country, than the funds which were expended to launch the National Guard and State Police into action for riot control in the Ferguson, Missouri incident. It should be noted that the TASER is not 100% reliable in stopping an unarmed suspect. What options in life are 100% reliable? It could, however, probably lower the number of police shootings of unarmed suspects if every officer in the country was provided this tool, in addition to handguns, for their defense.

Bryan de Klerk further explains it this way, "Bear in mind that more people were beaten to death with hands and feet than were killed by so-called assault rifles in 2012. Those victims were not allowed to use deadly force simply because their attacker did not have a weapon? I think not. Laws on self-defense seldom mention the use of a weapon. They are based on a reasonable fear that your life is in jeopardy, not the presence of a weapon in the hands of your attacker. The rise in popularity of Brazilian Jiu Jitsu and Mixed Martial Arts (MMA) style sports have also added new weapons to the attacker's hands only arsenal. Have you ever been choked out? In MMA sports, the defender can "tap out" or the referee can end the fight and pull the attacker off of you. In the real world you could be choked until you die."

Rule 7

"Flinch" Will Destroy Your Accuracy

"Flinch" is defined as to "make a quick, nervous movement of the face or body as an instinctive reaction to surprise, fear or pain." Flinching while shooting is the cause of most accuracy problems. You must engage in "dry fire" firearms practice on a regular basis to force your mind and body to be positively conditioned to not have the muscle memory "flinch" reaction to a loud explosion and recoil when you are shooting your firearm. Shooting live rounds actually conditions your mind and body to expect and anticipate the recoil of your pistol and may cause you to "flinch". Dry fire practice has the complete opposite effect on your brain and should therefore be conducted with more frequency than live fire training. If you are a firearms instructor, it is a mistake to immediately take your students to the range and have them fire high caliber heavy powder load ammunition before they have practiced dry firing their pistols. The reason for doing this is to avoid a first impression in the shooter's mind to always anticipate high recoil and a very loud explosion every time they pull the trigger. It conditions them from the very start of their training to develop a natural flinch response when they pull the trigger. Let me tell you a short story which helps to explain what I mean.

John is a good friend of mine who wanted to teach his wife, Chris, how to shoot a handgun. John is a Dallas Police Officer, so he believed it was important for his wife to be knowledgeable of handguns, but Chris did not like guns and had a fear of them. Chris, who had never fired a gun before in her life, was exceptionally nervous. John was patient and reassured her over and over, that with good training, she had nothing to worry about and pistols were actually fun to shoot. John did a thorough job of instructing her in all the basic gun safety rules along with providing good guidance about the proper grip, stance, sight picture, etc. He overlooked the high probability she would have a flinch reaction and failed to give her significant dry fire practice before he took her to the range on his parent's farm in Texas. John also made a big mistake by loading his .357 magnum S&W revolver with heavy powder load .357 magnum rounds, rather than low powder .38 special rounds in the revolver. Chris took careful aim at the bullseye target 25 yards in front of her.

She slowly squeezed the trigger as she had been trained. When the round ignited, it must have sounded like a cannon going off to Chris. She immediately screamed and dropped the revolver in front of her in shock. She had not anticipated the loud noise and powerful recoil of the weapon. She let her husband know, in no uncertain terms, that the experience was terrible and she never wanted to shoot a gun again, turned her back to him and ran back to their family farmhouse.

The amazing part of this story is that when I walked the 25 yards down the range to check her target, I discovered that she had hit a dead bullseye in the center of the target! For her first shot, her precision was superior to the vast majority of Dallas Police Officers that complete firearms training. Upon discovery of this remarkable shot, I told Chris that her shooting was actually magnificent, and she should return to the range to try it again using low powder .38 special loads. It took some significant cajoling to get Chris to return to the range, but when she finally did, for two days her shooting was terrible and she could rarely hit the target at any distance.

Why was it that her first shot was so magnificent, and then she had trouble even hitting a target at close range thereafter? The explanation is simple, if you know anything about firearms instruction. Chris had been trained well in the skills of marksmanship but her mind did not anticipate heavy recoil when she fired that first shot. It is the anticipation of the heavy recoil and loud noise, which causes your mind to react and your body to flinch. Her mind had not anticipated the noise and recoil, so after the shock of the experience, the imprint in her mind caused her to flinch in future attempts. So how do you train your mind not to tell your body to flinch? Dry fire practice is a good start, but there are also two other techniques I have found to be very useful.

You have to train your mind to accept that the recoil and loud noise from shooting a firearm will not hurt you. It is just a natural part of our parasympathetic nervous system to flinch or jump when you hear a loud noise next to you, but if you heard loud noises next to you frequently the reaction dulls significantly with time. This is just one reason why practice is so important for your mind and muscle memory, but we will get to that more in the next rule. "Dry firing" is the action of operating your firearm like you are shooting it, but the firearm is empty. If you follow a few simple steps, it is safe, causes no harm to your gun (unless it is one of the very older models) and is highly effective at improving your shooting skill. It's free, you can do it almost anywhere and anytime, you can monitor how you are doing without the noise or recoil to hide your mistakes, you can see your own flinch, and you don't have to go to the range to practice. Nothing will improve your shooting faster than spending five to ten minutes several times a week dry firing. There are two other techniques which I have found will help with flinch and improve your overall shooting skill.

The "Russian roulette" training technique is very effective at reducing your flinch. No, I am not talking about pointing the revolver at anyone's head and pulling the trigger, but it is similar to what you are thinking. It involves taking a revolver and only putting one or two rounds into the six round cylinder, spinning the cylinder before you close it so the student doesn't know which of the six pulls of the revolver trigger it will actually fire, then handing the revolver to your student to fire at the target on the range. You will be amazed how quickly this will help reduce flinch. You and the student both can observe his over-reaction flinch and barrel wiggle when he pulls the trigger on an empty cylinder. With time and practice, the student will self correct and eventually eliminate most, if not all, of his flinch.

The other technique that will help improve smooth trigger pull, as well as flinch, is the "Coin on the Barrel" training technique. This can be done with either a semi-auto pistol or a revolver and involves simply balancing a coin such as a penny, nickel or quarter on the front of the barrel of your pistol while you are conducting dry fire practice. If you have a very smooth trigger pull and no flinch, the coin will remain balanced on the top front of your barrel when you complete pulling the trigger and the hammer falls. Remember, the only part of your body that should move when you take a shot is the smooth pull of your trigger finger. If you are not doing this correctly, when you pull the trigger the coin will fall off the barrel. Practice will enable you to keep that coin on the barrel when you dry fire your handgun.

From left to right, the Coin on the Barrel and Russian Roulette techniques are shown

Rule 8

Firearms Shooting Fundamentals

In a gunfight, those who train, win. When the going gets tough, you will revert to your lowest level of training in that high stress deadly force situation. Building a home without a good foundation can have disastrous consequences. If you practice shooting firearms without knowledge of the basic shooting fundamentals you can develop bad habits and also have negative consequences. Habits are the mind's shortcuts. If we had to think through everything we do each time we did it, our days would be filled with reinventing each little movement, such as figuring out how to turn a doorknob every time we approached a door. The mind takes repetitive activities and creates an "automatic pilot" that imprints those things that we have already learned. If you do not want to take the time to learn how to be proficient with your firearm, it might be better for you not to have one. Pulling out a weapon that you are not trained to use could result in having it malfunction or being taken from you to become the tool of your own demise. You must learn and PRACTICE, PRACTICE, PRACTICE all of the proper techniques of muscle memory, proper stance, footing, handgun grip, arm & elbow lock, breathing techniques and sight picture. If you want accuracy, remember to always squeeze the trigger while controlling the movement of your body to just the smooth movement of your trigger finger to avoid barrel wiggle while taking a shot. It is important that your body remain completely stable once the shot breaks. Once you have memorized it properly, it is like riding a bicycle and you will not forget how to do it.As I mentioned in the introduction to this book, one of the best firearms instruction courses I ever attended was conducted by Dick Cook, an old Sheriff's Deputy in Abilene, Kansas, who was a quick draw expert and master of instinct shooting from the hip. He had a range set up in the "Old Abilene Town" tourist attraction.

Dick always shot from the hip without looking at his sights. At very close ranges of 15 feet or less, he was quicker and as accurate as any United States Practical Shooting Association (U.S.P.S.A.) or Olympic shooter I have ever observed. This type of instinct shooting technique is probably superior, at close range, to any firearms shooting technique I have ever observed. To be proficient in this type of instinct shooting technique, be prepared to spend hundreds of hours of practice. Nearly ninety percent of all pistol- shooting incidents occur at a range of 15 feet or less. This technique of hip or point shooting is only used in short-range situations; it loses accuracy in hitting targets at longer ranges. If you utilize cover, and maintain distance from your adversary, it greatly mitigates your chances of being hit by a hip-shooting expert as you are exposing such a small target, especially if your adversary is proficient in hip shooting. The hip shooting method is employed in quick-draw situations where the shooter may not have time to draw the firearm to eye level. A very similar technique of point shooting was also taught by Fairbarn, Sykes, and Applegate, who were involved in training some of the first commando forces during World War II.

The quick draw instinct shooting technique is rarely shown accurately in most old western movies. It is very rare to see competition shooters and police officers utilize the instinct or hip shooting technique because it is generally only used for close range. It has been proven that a fairly quick, very accurate, and sensible certain hit is better than a lightning fast miss. If you haven't mastered the instinct shooting technique properly, you will most likely miss. Most people definitely don't want to dedicate the significant time, money for extensive ammunition expenses, and the effort required to master instinct shooting. In addition, it is not something that you could really learn from reading a book like this. Don't worry that you aren't going to become a master of instinct shooting from reading this book, as I doubt that any of the common street thug bad guys you run into on the street will have the opportunity, or the discipline, to learn it. It is true that some people are naturally good shots, but in reality the vast majority of us would have to spend hundreds of hours of practice to get even close to the instinct shooting expertise displayed in the movie *Django Unchained*. Therefore, what I am going to do is provide you with the next best thing. Explain some of the best combat techniques, aside from close range instinct hip shooting, for firearms shooting proficiency.

Proper Stance & Footing

The Isosceles and Weaver shooting stances are probably the two most popular types of shooting stances. There is much debate in the law enforcement community about which stance is better from a tactical perspective. Years ago the Weaver stance was taught to most Police Officers. The idea was that you presented slightly less of a target if you were bladed to the bad guy, but when bladed, you run the risk of a round striking you in the gap between the front and back panels of your ballistic vest. Today, many law enforcement firearms Instructors see the need for the Isosceles stance. Most police officers wear a department issued ballistic vest. I have seen some police departments switch to the Isosceles stance as some feel it is easier to train and more stable. The object of squaring up with the bad guy is to align your body so the vest will catch the bullet should you be hit. On the other side of the debate, some argue that by facing the target directly, you expose your groin, both femoral arteries and a larger overall profile to hit.

To say I am exposing one armpit by doing the Weaver, is countered by the fact that the Isosceles exposes your dominant side shoulder more. If you are hit there, your dominant arm is out of the ball game. In the Weaver, the dominant side shoulder is harder to hit.

I see advantages and disadvantages to both shooting stances, and would recommend that you try them both and see which works better for you. In my opinion, the bottom line is which one you, as an individual, are more accurate with. Of course, you are probably not going to be able to learn either stance properly by just reading this book. It would be best to go to the range and get guidance from a qualified instructor and practice. Do your research on the shooting school you plan to attend. You want a course that has instructors which will train you to have good tactics, as well as firearms accuracy.

The Weaver Stance

The Weaver stance was utilized at police academies across the world for many years. In the Weaver stance your body takes up a bladed body position, with the strong side foot placed to the rear and the body bladed at approximately 45 degrees to the target. The arms create isometric pressure with the strong arm slightly flexed and pushing forward, with the support arm elbow down, and pulling back.

The Isosceles Stance

The Isosceles stance gets its name from the fact your body is forming a perfect triangle by the straight arms and squared shoulders of the stance. Your body directly faces the target as you have both arms fully extended and pointed directly at the target. The stance is designed to face an attacker head on and to push the arms out defensively and square up to the target. In addition, since both arms are at full extension, recoil is easily managed. The shooter will find the firearm dropping back on target immediately after the muzzle rise. Since the arms point directly at the target using the Isosceles, it also provides a simple method of using unsighted fire in a stress situation.

In the distant past, many police departments actually trained police officers to shoot one handed in a manner similar to what you see in current Olympic shooting events, with your body completely turned sideways to your target. This is the style of shooting which was used in duels with flintlock pistols in centuries past. It could be very accurate if practiced by a professional for hours, but I do not recommend this type of one handed shooting for combat situations. The vast majority of shooters are much faster and more accurate shooting with two hands compared to one; however, this type of shooting technique is not without value. I would recommend that everyone spend at least a small portion of your shooting time in practice shooting with only one hand. If you are ever shot in your strong hand or arm, you can transition your weapon to the hand/arm which is not injured and the training will give you some familiarization in shooting with only one hand.

The **Burr–Hamilton** duel was a duel with flintlock pistols between two prominent American politicians. The former Secretary of the Treasury Alexander Hamilton was killed by the sitting Vice President Aaron Burr on July 11, 1804.

Handgun Grip

There are scores of articles written on the proper handgun grip for revolvers and semi-auto pistols, but a picture says a thousand words. Therefore, for the purposes of simplicity, I have illustrated the proper grip with accompanying photos and comments.

When shooting a semi-auto pistol the two-handed hold, above, is the best hold to utilize. The supporting hand is cupped over the strong hand and your fingers are laid over those gripping the pistol to form a platform under the trigger guard. The thumb of the supporting hand is placed over or alongside that of the strong hand. The supporting hand's thumb must not be placed across the back of the wrist of the strong hand where it can be struck by the cycling of the slide during firing.

The above photograph of a two-handed revolver grip is fine if you are shooting a revolver (thumb of left hand over top of right wrist), but could result in injury to your left thumb if you tried to utilize this technique with a semi-auto pistol. The slide of the semi-auto pistol would recoil to the rear, to feed the next round into the chamber, and could cut your left thumb during this process.

When shooting a revolver you have two types of holds you can utilize. When you shoot a two-handed revolver hold, the grip of the shooting hand is unchanged from what is noted above for a semi-auto pistol hold. You still use your supporting hand to simply cup around the strong hand, applying pressure to provide a steady platform to control the trigger. The option is to place the thumb of the supporting hand on top of the strong hand or laid across the back of the wrist. From either position, the supporting hand thumb can be used to cock the hammer for single-action fire.

The two handed grip is the best choice in any situation. The first step is to place your pistol correctly in your strong hand. The placement of the strong hand stays the same regardless of a semi- auto pistol or a revolver. The support hand is wrapped around the strong hand, as shown above, with the thumb lapped over the strong hand thumb. When firing the pistol, the strong arm should be stiff, with the support hand pulling back slightly against the shooting hand. The push-pull action steadies the hands and wrists and gives a strong aiming platform for firing the handgun.

Arm, Elbow & Wrist Lock

There are several things that cause the sights to become misaligned. The wrist not being held in a stationary position is one. To eliminate this, concentrate on getting the arm straight with the elbow locked and by gripping the gun as hard as you can grip without it starting to tremble. Imagine that you are holding a living bird in your shooting hand that you don't want to fly away. You need to put a strong grip on it, but not so strong that you crush the bird and kill it.

Proper Breathing

Let us discuss how to breathe to achieve the best accuracy while shooting a firearm. Consistency is very important for accurate shooting. Under stress, you will shoot in the manner you have trained. You have probably observed that when you take position to shoot and you breathe, your sights move up and down slightly as your diaphragm moves up and down. This affects your elevation and the point of impact of your bullets. When I was a young man, learning how to shoot my first .22 caliber rifle, I was told that the best breathing technique for shooting was "take a deep breath, let half your deep breath out, then hold your breath and take the shot." This was not bad advice, but there is another technique that is better. You want to be at your best when you break the shot, but that can be affected by how much oxygen is in your system, and holding your breathe for longer than a few seconds can be detrimental to your shooting. After five to seven seconds, your oxygen level goes down and this can harm your performance. In fact, the longer you hold your breath, the worse it gets.

The "natural respiratory pause" is the best technique to utilize and train with. Your diaphragm moves up and down as you breathe. When the diaphragm contracts, it causes your lungs to expand and take in air. When it relaxes, you expel air and no pushing or tension is needed to get that air out, this is your natural respiratory pause and the time to shoot. Inhale, then relax and let your breath escape naturally, take a good sight picture and get ready to fire. You should then take the shot within three seconds. If you still haven't sighted in on your target, take another breath and start over.

Sight Picture

The first thing you need to do before you start working on your sight picture, is to ascertain which of your eyes is the dominant or "shooting eye". It may seem strange but a few people who are right handed are actually left eye dominant and vice versa. There is a simple test you can conduct to see which eye is dominant. With both eyes open, pick an object in the room and raise your hand up to point at it. Now, freeze that hand and finger in the air, do not move your hand or body, and keep your finger frozen in the air and pointed at that object. Close your left eye, and then your right eye. You will see that you are still pointing at the object directly with one eye, but not the other. The eye that still sees the object directly in front of your finger, when the other eye is closed, is your dominant or shooting eye. When you close your dominant eye, the other eye sees your finger pointing slightly to the left or right of the object. While we are on the subject of your eyes and shooting, I also want to point out that you are better off if you can learn to keep both eyes open when shooting. The reason for this is because it gives you better peripheral vision to see if another target, when you are hunting or in a self-defense situation, is approaching from the side of your closed eye. Many people like to close one eye when shooting as they feel it helps them to focus better. I am right eye dominant, so when I shoot I squint my left eye, but do not close it completely. This allows me to maintain my peripheral vision, and works well because it also seems to subconsciously immediately tell my mind which eye to focus for shooting. Keeping both eyes open is something every shooter should strive for. Muscle memory through countless hours of repetition is the key to overcoming a "one eye closed" problem.

Proper Sight Alignment + sight picture	Proper Sight Alignment but off target	Front sight on target, but bad sight alignment
		Aligned Left / Aligned Low

Shot Placement

SIGHT ALIGNMENT

REAR SIGHT   FRONT SIGHT

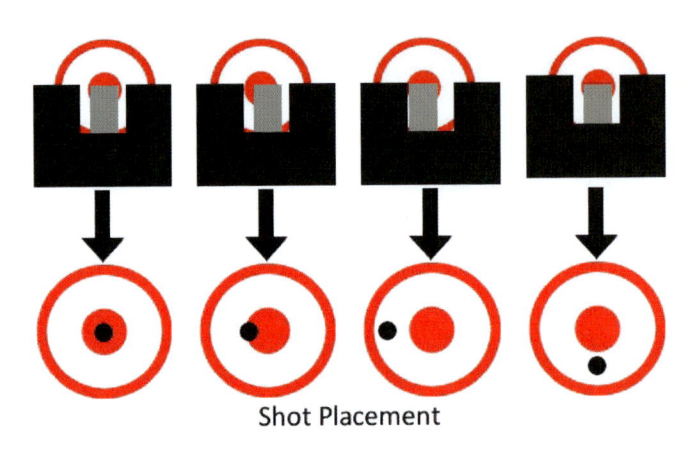

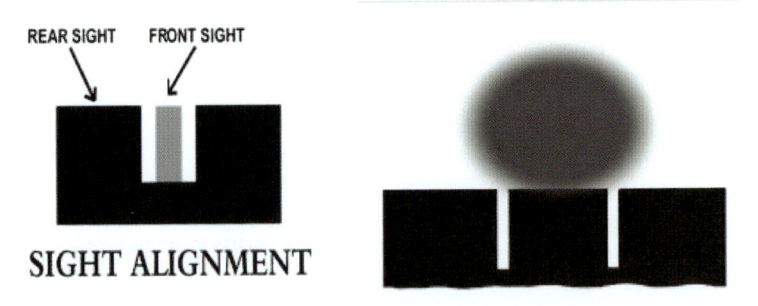

The focus of your shooting eye should be on the front and rear sights of your firearm with the target just slightly blurred, as shown in the above photographs.

Right Hand Correction Chart
Adapted to NRA B3 size from the U.S. Army Marksmanship Training Guide

- Breaking Wrist Up
- Pushing (Anticipating Recoil) or No Follow Through
- Heeling (Anticipating Recoil)
- Too little trigger finger
- Thumbing (squeezing thumb) or Too much trigger finger
- Tightening Fingers
- Tightening Grip while Pulling Trigger
- Jerking or Slapping Trigger
- Breaking Wrist Down, Pushing Forward, or Drooping Head

The photograph shown above illustrates the shot placement groups and what the corresponding problems are when firing the weapon.

Improper Shooting Techniques

Now that you know what you should do for firearms accuracy, let's talk about a couple techniques you shouldn't utilize, but frequently see in movies. How many times have you seen police officers and bad guys in the movies hold a handgun immediately next to the head of someone? If you do this, yes, you have undoubtedly totally intimidated them and will certainly hit them if you pull the trigger, but you have also dramatically increased the odds your adversary might be able to disarm you! Proper distance from your adversary is very important and we will discuss this more in RULE 12.

The other ill advised shooting technique you frequently see in movies, but is dangerous to utilize in real life, is to shoot with your handgun pointed sideways as shown below. For some unknown reason gang bangers think it is really cool to shoot a pistol like this. Both fortunately and unfortunately, bad guys frequently utilize this stupid shooting technique when involved in crimes. It is fortunate in that they are usually very poor shots when they utilize this technique. It is unfortunate in that they are frequently such bad shots that innocent bystanders and children are often killed by stray bullets during their robbery attempts and drive by shootings.

Rule 9

Weapon Advantage

The difference between a professional and an amateur is that the professional stacks the odds in his favor. Rifles and shotguns are superior to handguns and more accurate, especially in long- range gunfights, and they have better stopping power than pistols. Just as you wouldn't bring a knife to a gunfight, if you have a choice, don't bring just a pistol, if your adversary has a rifle or shotgun. For those of you who are hunters, or have served in the military, this rule will seem like some very basic common sense that you would assume almost everyone should know. You would be surprised how many people from large urban areas don't understand the difference between the rifle, shotgun and pistol capabilities in real gunfights.

Many people also assume that all police officers and military personnel are experts with all three types of firearms (pistols, rifles, and shotguns). The truth is that all police officers receive training with their department issued pistols, along with a small amount of training with shotguns, but the vast majority of police departments do not provide formal rifle training. The exceptions to this are the Special Weapons and Tactics (SWAT) Teams. With the military, the situation is almost the complete reverse. Every U.S. Army soldier and U.S. Marine receives excellent training with the M-16 rifle and more than likely will receive minimal training with pistols and shotguns unless he is assigned to the military police or is an officer in the military. The military knows that pistols are not nearly as accurate, especially at ranges beyond 30 yards, or as effective at stopping the enemy, as rifles. Pistols are viewed as a weapon of last resort in the military because they know, even at close range, it probably would take 2 or more rounds from a pistol, to have the same takedown power as one well placed round from a 5.56 or 7.62 caliber rifle. High-powered rifles have a much higher relative incapacitation index because of the heavy powder load and the longer barrel which enables much higher velocity of the bullet than a short barrel pistol. It is noted that most pistol bullets are not traveling fast enough to produce major temporary cavities that damage tissue as a high caliber rifle bullet would. The temporary cavity of a pistol bullet is generally smaller and also formed at a much slower speed which causes less damage. One must also consider that human tissue has elastic properties, tissue will stretch a lot, and if impacted at slower speeds, it might not tear as significantly.

Many people also assume that if you are a good shot with a rifle, you are probably a good shot with a pistol and/or shotgun. The truth is that there is a small amount of carryover, but I have known expert rifle shots who were just average or even poor shots with a pistol or shotgun. Good pistol shots are usually at least fairly good with a rifle, but sometimes incompetent with a shotgun at fast moving targets. Shotgun experts are the best at hitting moving targets as they know how to swing and provide lead into the moving target (this only makes sense as shotguns are used for trap shooting & bird hunting), but some of the shotgun experts are just average shots with a pistol or rifle. All three types of firearms have similarities, but are different skill sets. You may be a great sports car driver, but this doesn't mean you know how to race a motorcycle or drive a bulldozer. If you want to be prepared to defend yourself in any type of gunfight, you should have at least a basic familiarization with all three types of weapons on the range. I want to relate a story about a shootout in Florida which demonstrates how superior rifles are to pistols, giving domestic law enforcement a big wakeup call. Many of the specific details of this shooting incident were related to me during an officer survival program at Quantico, but some are paraphrased from Wikipedia's reports of the incident:

The 1986 FBI Miami shootout was a gun battle that occurred on April 11, 1986 in south Florida between eight FBI agents and two serial bank robbers. During the firefight, FBI Special Agents Jerry

L. Dove and Benjamin P. Grogan were killed, while five other FBI agents were wounded. The highly successful FBI had never seen this type of costly semi-defeat in a gun battle before. Fortunately, the two armed robbery suspects, William Russell Matix and Michael Lee Platt, were also killed. The incident is infamous in FBI history and is well-studied in law enforcement circles. Despite outnumbering the suspects 4 to 1, the agents found themselves pinned down by rifle fire and unable to respond effectively. Although both Matix and Platt were hit multiple times during the firefight, Platt fought on and continued to injure and kill agents. The FBI agents involved in this gunfight were good shots but had inferior weapons. None of them had rifles in this unusual and relatively long-range gunfight. They hit the suspects numerous times with their 9-millimeter pistols and .357 magnum revolver rounds, but the suspects still lived long enough to kill and injure several of them. The suspects in this case were very different from your normal bank robbery suspects. Matix first served in the U.S. Marine Corps from 1969 to 1972 and was later honorably discharged after reaching the rank of Staff Sergeant. In 1973, Matix enlisted in the U.S. Army and served in the military police and was honorably discharged from the Army in 1976. Platt enlisted in 1972 as an infantryman and served with the U.S. Army Rangers during the Vietnam War where he was noted for "High Combat Proficiency". These men were expert rifle shots and active target shooters who had spent countless hours of time and thousands of rounds of ammunition practicing shooting high caliber rifles, even after the completion of their tours of military duty.

The FBI agents initiated a rolling stakeout for the black Monte Carlo the suspects were believed to be driving on April 11, 1986, but they did not know the identity or the military background of the suspects at the time. They were acting on a hunch that the pair would attempt a robbery that morning. A total of fourteen FBI agents in eleven cars participated in the search, but only eight of these agents took part in the actual shootout. The other six agents involved in the stakeout, who did not reach the shootout in time to participate, did have additional weaponry including Remington shotguns, Heckler & Koch MP5 submachine guns, and M-16 rifles.

Around 9:30 am., agents Grogan and Dove spotted the suspect vehicle and began to follow it. Two other stakeout team cars joined them, and an attempt to make a felony traffic stop of the suspects was conducted before the rest of the FBI agents arrived at the scene. The suspects were forced off the road following collisions with the FBI cars. This sent the suspect's car nose first into a tree in front of a house at 12201 Southwest 82nd Avenue, pinned against a parked car on the passenger side and an FBI vehicle on the driver side. Of the eight FBI agents at the scene, two had shotguns in their vehicles, three were armed with S&W 9mm pistols, and the rest were armed with S&W revolvers. Two of the agents had backup revolvers they would utilize at some point during the gunfight.

The initial collision that forced the suspects off the road caused some unforeseen problems for the agents, as the FBI vehicles sustained damage from the heavier, older car driven by Matix. Just prior to ramming the Monte Carlo, one of the agents had pulled out his service revolver and placed it on the seat in anticipation of a shootout, but the force of the collision flung open his door and sent his weapon flying. Another agent lost his .357 magnum service revolver during the initial collision, though he was still able to fight with his backup gun. The collision knocked off FBI agent Grogan's eyeglasses, and there is speculation his vision was so bad that he was unable to see clearly enough to be effective. Grogan, however, is credited with landing the first hit of the gunfight, wounding Matix in the forearm as he leaned out of the Monte Carlo to fire a shotgun at Grogan & Dove.

One of the FBI agents was wounded when Platt fired several rounds from his Mini-14 rifle that penetrated the door of FBI agent Manauzzi's car, something a pistol probably would not be able to do. Another FBI agent fired over the hood of his car but was wounded by return fire from Platt's more accurate rifle. Platt then fired his rifle at a third agent who was running across the street to join the fight. This agent was hit in the left forearm, creating a severe wound. Platt then pulled back from the window, giving Matix opportunity to fire. Due to collision damage, Matix could only open his door partially, and fired one shotgun round at Grogan and Dove, striking their vehicle. Matix was then shot in the right forearm, probably by Grogan. FBI agent McNeill returned fire with six shots from his revolver, hitting Matix with two rounds in the head and neck. Matix was apparently knocked unconscious by the hits and fired no more rounds. FBI agent McNeill was then shot in the hand, and due to his wound and blood in his revolver's chambers, could not reload. The fact so many FBI agents were shot in the hand or forearm, or their pistol was hit, gives the indication they were tactically sound in utilizing cover (where only the hands, gun, and shooting eye are exposed as a target). While that small target area is very difficult to hit with a pistol at any range, it would not be that difficult for an expert rifle marksman to score a hit on the small target, especially when only a few yards away.

As Platt climbed out of the passenger side car window, one of Dove's 9 mm rounds hit his right upper arm and went on to penetrate his chest, stopping an inch away from his heart. The autopsy found Platt's right lung was collapsed and his chest cavity contained 1.3 liters of blood, suggesting damage to the main blood vessels of the right lung. Of his many gunshot wounds, this was the primary injury responsible for Platt's eventual death. The car had come to a stop against a parked vehicle, and Platt had to climb across the hood of this vehicle. As he did so, he was shot a second and third time, in the right thigh and left foot. The shots were believed to have been fired by FBI agent Dove.

Platt fired two rounds from his Mini-14 rifle at two other FBI agent positions wounding FBI agent Orrantia with shrapnel created by the bullet's passage, and fired two rounds at agent McNeill. One round hit McNeill in the neck, causing him to collapse and leaving him paralyzed for several hours. Platt then apparently positioned the Mini-14 against his shoulder using his uninjured left hand. FBI agent Dove's 9 mm pistol was rendered inoperative after being hit by one of Platt's bullets. Another FBI agent fired at Platt and was shot in the hand while reloading. Grogan and Dove were kneeling alongside the driver's side of their car. Both were preoccupied with getting Dove's gun working and did not detect that Platt was aggressively advancing upon them. Platt rounded the rear of their car and killed Grogan with a shot to the chest, shot Hanlon in the groin area, and then killed Dove with two shots to the head. Platt then entered the Grogan/Dove car in an apparent attempt to flee the scene. As Platt entered Grogan and Dove's car, FBI agent Mireles, able to use only one arm, fired the first of five rounds from his pump action shotgun, wounding Platt in both feet. At an unknown time, Matix had regained consciousness and he joined Platt in the car, entering via the passenger door. Mireles fired four more rounds at Platt and Matix, but hit neither.

Platt attempted to start the Grogan/Dove car. Mireles drew his .357 Magnum revolver, moved parallel to the street and then directly toward Platt and Matix. Mireles fired six rounds at the suspects. The first round missed, hitting the back of the front seat. The second hit the driver's side window post and fragmented, with one small piece hitting Platt in the scalp. The third hit Matix in the face, and fragmented in two, with neither piece causing a serious wound. The fourth hit Matix in the face next to his right eye socket, travelled downward through the facial bones, into the neck, where it entered the spinal column and severed the spinal cord. The fifth hit Matix in the face, penetrated the jaw bone and neck and came to rest by the spinal column. Mireles then reached the driver's side door, extended his revolver through the window, and fired his sixth shot at Platt. The bullet penetrated Platt's chest and bruised the spinal cord, ending the gunfight.

The shootout involved ten people: two suspects and eight FBI agents. Of the ten, only one, Special Agent Manauzzi, did not fire any shots (his firearm was thrown from his car in the initial collision), while only one, Special Agent Risner, was able to emerge from the battle without a wound. The incident lasted under five minutes yet approximately 145 shots were exchanged. Toxicology tests showed that the abilities of Platt and Matix to fight through multiple traumatic gunshot wounds and continue to battle and attempt to escape were not achieved through any chemical means. Both of their bodies were drug-free at the time of their deaths.

The subsequent FBI investigation placed partial blame for the agents' deaths on the lack of stopping power exhibited by their service handguns, but it is the author's opinion that anytime you try to compete against rifles with pistols you are at a distinct disadvantage with regard to accuracy at any distance, as well as stopping power. Other issues were brought up in the aftermath of the shooting. Despite being on the lookout for two violent felons who were known to use firearms during their crimes, only two of the FBI vehicles contained shotguns (in addition to Mireles, McNeill had a shotgun in his car, but he was unable to reach it before the shootout began), and none of the agents were armed with rifles. Only two of the agents were wearing ballistic vests, and the armor they were wearing was standard light body armor, which is designed to protect against handgun rounds, not the .223 Remington rounds fired by Platt's Mini-14

Ruger rifle. While heavier armor providing protection against rifle rounds would normally have been hot and uncomfortable to wear on patrol in Miami's April climate, the agents spending the day sitting in air conditioned vehicles on the lookout for a single target were facing more ideal conditions for its use.

There are several tactical issues to be learned from this legendary firefight. It was the first time, in my memory, the police had suffered such significant multiple losses in a single gunfight since the old gangster era of the 1920's and 1930's when the bad guys like Machine Gun Kelley and Clyde Barker of "Bonnie & Clyde" fame carried Tommy Guns and BAR high powered rifles. Some Americans think the police are over-reacting as they now frequently send SWAT teams with high powered rifles and sub- machine gun weapons to respond to emergencies, but incidents such as this one show they are only prudent to do so.

Another one of the longest and bloodiest police shootouts in U.S. police history took place in Los Angeles on February 28, 1997. The "North Hollywood Shootout" was a gunfight between the Los Angeles Police Department (LAPD) and two bank robbers who were armed with ballistic vests and automatic rifles with high capacity drum magazines. Both robbers were killed after a long gunfight, eleven police officers and seven civilians were injured, and numerous vehicles and other property were damaged or destroyed by the nearly 2,000 rounds of ammunition fired by the armed robbers and the police. The police who initially engaged the suspects were armed with only 9 mm and .38 caliber pistols, with some having a 12-gauge shotgun available in their cars. The suspects wore heavy body armor which successfully deflected pistol bullets and shotgun pellets fired by the responding patrolmen. A Special Weapons and Tactics (SWAT)Team armed with AR-15 rifles eventually arrived and saved the day. Several officers also ran to a nearby gun store and appropriated AR-15 rifles when they realized the pistols and shotguns were having little effect on the suspects with heavy body armor. The suspects could be wounded in their legs and hands, but the robbers' heads were the only vital organs that were unprotected. The LAPD officers' service pistols had insufficient range and poor accuracy for a long- range gunfight.

Why A Shotgun or Rifle Round Is Better Than A Pistol Round?

The answer is simple physics. The kinetic energy equation $KE = \frac{1}{2}mv^2$ *(m=mass, v=velocity)*. Compare the energy of a shotgun to a couple common pistol calibers and the .223 rifle at the muzzle. The powder type, amount and grain weight of the bullet all could be factored in to influence the numbers listed below, but you get the idea. Refer to Table 1 for comparisons of different rounds and their associated energy outputs.

Round	Energy
.380 ACP Pistol	203 ft./lbs.
.45 ACP Pistol	250 ft./lbs.
.223 Remington Rifle	1310 ft./lbs.
12 Gauge Shotgun, 00 buckshot (1.107 oz. load)	1547 ft./lbs.

Table 1

The Shotgun

In response to the Sandy Hook Elementary School shooting, Vice President Biden gave some very poor advice when he talked about how a woman should just shoot a double barrel shotgun in the air on her back porch to scare away criminals, but there was some wisdom in his advice with regard to the weapon he recommended. Unless your adversary is wearing a bulletproof vest, it is the author's opinion that a high capacity shotgun with an extended tube magazine is the most deadly and effective weapon to utilize in any gunfight in ranges of 30 yards or less. I would rather have a reliable semi-auto shotgun with 00 buck load for close range combat than even a machine gun or any assault rifle in the world, especially if you are shooting at moving targets. The exception is if the suspect is wearing a bulletproof vest which would be more difficult for a shotgun to penetrate than a rifle, but how often do most street thugs wear a ballistic vest? The military rarely utilizes shotguns, unless you are in a jungle environment, because most of their firefights usually involve longer distances and multiple adversaries which mandate high capacity magazines and long range accuracy. In contrast, police officers and the armed citizen will rarely face more than one or two adversaries and these deadly force encounters are almost always at very close range.

An article by firearms expert John M. Buol stated the following: "Which long gun is superior for general defensive use: a carbine or a shotgun? The Joint Service Combat Shotgun (JSCS) program, led by the Marine Corps in the 1990's reported on the lethality of shotguns, noting that 'the probability of hitting a man- sized target with a shotgun was superior to that of all other weapons.' Their study determined that, to a range of 30 yards, the probability of hitting a man-sized target with a shotgun was better than other weapons. The probability of hitting an intended target with an assault rifle was one in eleven. It was one in eight with a submachine gun firing a five round burst. Shotguns had a hit probability ratio twice as good as rifles. Despite having a lower cartridge capacity, shotguns can put out a considerable payload. A submachine-gun armed SWAT entry man might be able to dump two magazines (60 rounds) into targets at room distance (15 feet or so) in under eight seconds. A competent shooter with a semi- automatic shotgun and an extended tube magazine (nine buckshot loads) unleashes nine .33 caliber, 00 buck pellets at 1,000 feet per second with each trigger pull, and can put that entire payload of projectiles onto the same targets in under three seconds."

Don't put the image of the more aggressive macho perception of carrying an assault rifle in preference to the practicality of a shotgun. Like every rule there are some exceptions, such as if you are one of those people (small frame female, the elderly, or handicapped) who can't handle the heavy recoil of a shotgun for self-defense, then get an AR-15 carbine. If you need a firearm for long range shooting, then yes, certainly get a rifle, but if you are looking for home defense at close range and can handle the heavy recoil, get a shotgun loaded with 00 or #1 buckshot shells.

    I always demanded that at least one of the narcotics agents in the groups I supervised should be armed with a shotgun when conducting drug raids. One of the reasons for this was because the methamphetamine labs they raided frequently had guard dogs (aggressive Pit Bulls & Rottweilers) to guard the location. These dogs can be shot several times with a pistol (if you are able to hit them in the first place when the dogs are rapidly charging you) and still bite the police officers raiding the location before the pistol rounds could stop them. Keep in mind that at least 4.5 to 4.7 million Americans are bitten by dogs every year, and there were at least 26 fatal dog attacks in 2000. The vast majority of the attacks do not result in death, according to the Centers for Disease Control and Prevention (CDC), which published a special report on the subject in 2000. I love dogs and hate to see them shot. A fire extinguisher works well to scare off the aggressive dogs, but that doesn't always work and the police are sometimes forced to shoot the dogs. The shotgun is much more efficient than pistols and usually stops the dogs immediately. An aggressive dog can move like a bat out of hell and is sometimes very difficult to hit with a pistol. If you don't believe me, try going bird hunting or trap shooting with a pistol and see how many of those fast moving targets you hit.

Do you want to have a pistol, or a shotgun, when this dog is running at you at 30 miles per hour?

Rule 10

Tombstone Courage, The "Dirty Harry Syndrome"

The U.S. Special Forces have a saying that "Individuals Perish, but Teams Survive!" Teamwork should almost always take precedence over individual initiative. No matter how skilled or tough you may think you are, there will always be someone better, and if not some individual, it will be a group, or simple bad luck, which will eventually bring your demise if you always act alone. This is why teamwork is essential to have your highest level of safety in a deadly force encounter. Don't try to be Rambo or develop the "Dirty Harry" syndrome and try to be the Lone Ranger. Whether you are a civilian who has just found their house broken into, or a police officer responding to an emergency, always call for police backup and never enter a building alone to confront a suspect by yourself, unless mandated by exigent circumstances. This applies to physical assault situations as much as to deadly force firearms situations. If you have a suspicious person lurking in the dark outside your home, do not go outside by yourself and confront him with a gun or you could find yourself in a Trayvon Martin situation where you possibly have to wrestle to maintain your gun, and thereby might even end up in a shooting situation which could have been avoided. You might even end up finding yourself on trial. Why not wait for the police, or at least bring one or two other men with you? Most criminals are predators who will be reticent to attack if outnumbered.

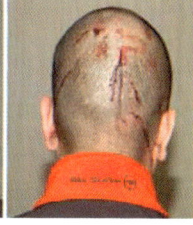

The Old West days of "One riot, one Texas Ranger" are over if you are a prudent police officer or armed citizen, especially if you live in an urban area where police back up in a major emergency should be able to arrive within minutes. Many of us have been influenced by the Hollywood movies which show the action hero of the show frequently confronting violent criminals by themselves and never call for backup. Sometimes you might see them call for back-up, but then they still march forward to confront violent criminals before that backup arrives and engage in one gunfight after another, and, of course, in the movies they almost always win. In the real world, police officers are frequently reprimanded for taking action by themselves or entering a building with a burglar alone to confront a suspect before their back-up arrived, unless there was some type of exigent circumstances which demanded immediate action. These rules exist because many police officers have been killed because they investigated crimes alone, and some of these deaths could have been avoided had they waited for other officers to arrive and support them. I could relate numerous real life examples of this, but I will explain with an example from a Hollywood movie I am sure most of you have seen, and will therefore have a better visual understanding of the background and details of the situation.

In the blockbuster hit movie *Silence of the Lambs*, FBI Special Agent Clarice Starling (played by Jodie Foster) is the protagonist and heroine of the story. Her talent as an investigator enables her to locate a serial killer named Buffalo Bill while she is in Belvedere, Ohio conducting interviews. She unknowingly stumbles onto the killer himself after knocking on the door to his home. She is alone and has not notified the FBI or local police where she is located. During the interview with the killer, she sees a Death Head moth flying in the house, the same rare type of moth the serial killer stuffs in the throats of each of his victims, and she now knows that she has found her man and tries to arrest him. Upon the realization her interview suspect is the actual serial killer, she draws her weapon and badge and tells Buffalo Bill to freeze, but Buffalo Bill runs around the corner in his home before she can get a shot at him. Buffalo Bill flees, and Agent Starling follows him into his basement, where his latest victim is alive and screaming for help. Buffalo Bill turns off the electricity in the basement, and stalks Starling through the rooms of the basement wearing night vision goggles and holding a pistol. He is about to shoot her when she hears a noise behind her and opens fire into the darkness, killing Buffalo Bill. The victim is rescued and Agent Starling is the heroine of the case. Is Hollywood FBI Agent Starling really a brilliant heroine, or tactically very stupid, but lucky? What mistakes, if any, do you think Agent Starling made in this attempted arrest?

I know the way the story is written makes for great Hollywood drama, but in real life I would have recommended Agent Starling receive a written reprimand if she was one of the federal agents under my supervision. I would have also recommended a commendation for her investigative skills, but her officer survival tactics were terrible and she should be sent back to the FBI Academy for more defensive tactics instruction. Agent Starling violated the first survival rule of this book, *Rule 1 Preparation* (she had no flashlight, but chased the suspect into the dark basement), but much more important she violated survival *Rule 10 Tombstone Courage*. Agent Starling is a relatively small female agent attempting to arrest a large, muscular male suspect who is a known serial killer, by herself, with no backup, and even failed to call for support. After the suspect runs and does not surrender, she further compounds her lack of wisdom by chasing him into a dark basement without a flashlight in her possession. In the movie, Buffalo Bill is about to shoot Agent Starling when she hears a noise behind her and opens fire into the darkness, killing Buffalo Bill. In the real world, that noise behind her could have been the kidnap victim or any innocent citizen. How did she know who it was since she couldn't see him, yet she fired into the darkness? Because it was Hollywood, it happened to be the bad guy behind her.

You place yourself in a huge position of tactical disadvantage when you chase a suspect into his own home for numerous reasons. You have no familiarity whatsoever with the suspects home. You have no idea where he has weapons or booby traps hidden. You have no idea what areas of cover and concealment he may be hiding behind while waiting to ambush you. Action is always quicker than reaction, so all he has to do is hide behind a couch and pop up with a handgun or shotgun to ambush you as you run through a room. He will have the drop on you to fire the first shot. I know what some of you Hollywood movie fans are now thinking, "Well, what would you have done?"

The prudent course of action was simple, but would certainly make a less dramatic Hollywood script. When Agent Starling saw the Death Head moth flying in the house and realized this man was the serial killer, she should have simply made some creative excuse to cut the interview short and exit the house as soon as possible. Instead of attempting to be a hero with "TOMBSTONE COURAGE", she should have immediately exited the house, and upon return to her vehicle she should have called the local police who would be much closer, as well as the FBI, to surround the house in an emergency status to make certain the suspect could not escape. Keep in mind that no one even knew where she was located. If she had failed in her attempt to arrest the suspect and save the kidnap victim, she would be dead and both the police and FBI would have no lead whatsoever concerning who the suspect was or where he was located. In the real world, if an FBI agent followed the course of action of Agent Starling in this film, the agent would probably be dead, and the FBI would not have a clue where she was located.

Rule 11

Never Give Up The Fight Or Your Gun

Never give up the fight or your gun! There are exceptions to every rule, but I have seen few circumstances where giving up your weapon and surrendering, because the bad guy had the drop on you, or you ran out of ammunition, resulted in a positive outcome. Depending on your distance from your adversary and the ability to run behind cover, you might be better off to take your chances and simply run like hell than surrender, as moving targets are much more difficult to shoot with a pistol. In the military battlefield, surrender might be a prudent option in some cases, but when you are dealing with violent predator criminals I would not expect to receive mercy, or any treatment in accordance with the Geneva Convention.

If you ask the average police officer or federal agent if they would ever surrender their firearm their answer will probably be "NEVER". Part of the reason for this is because many officers have been trained to never give up their weapon. Read Joseph Wambaugh's book "The Onion Field", and learn lessons from this tragic incident that took place back in 1963. In this book, two LAPD officers named Hettinger and Campbell stopped a vehicle because of suspicious activity. Unknown to these officers, the occupants of the vehicle had been involved in a rash of armed robberies. Campbell was taken hostage at gunpoint and Hettinger was ordered by the suspects, and his own partner, to surrender his weapon. Hettinger did surrender his weapon and they were then driven to an onion field near Bakersfield, CA, where Campbell was murdered, but Hettinger ran and escaped into the darkness of the night.

This incident resulted in huge humiliation for Hettinger, who was forced to go from one police precinct to another in the LAPD to explain how he had screwed up and gotten his partner killed. He eventually suffered Post Traumatic Stress Disorder and was eventually fired. After this incident, many law enforcement agencies trained their officers to follow the following guidelines:
- Carry backup weapons
- Have a pre-determined plan if a partner is taken hostage
- Remember that if you have a tactical advantage, keep it
- And NEVER give up your gun

As general guidelines, these rules are prudent. I emphasize there are exceptions to every rule, and I would hesitate to criticize anyone who failed to follow them in certain situations, as this is a judgment call and every situation is different. There have been incidents where police officers surrendered their weapons and survived, but unfortunately they are few. I normally encourage officers to maintain control of their weapons and not rely on the bad guy's mercy, but it is difficult to Monday morning quarterback when you know the bad guy had the drop on the officer, the officer is outnumbered or outgunned, and the officer has just a few seconds to make that kind of decision. Psychology experts estimate that as many as 20% of currently incarcerated prisoners are psychopaths. Psychopaths feel no empathy or guilt and are therefore highly unlikely to show you any mercy should you surrender to them. Serial Killer Ted Bundy is quoted as saying, "I don't feel guilty for anything. I feel sorry for people who feel guilt." Psychopaths are master manipulators who can appear to be very charming and empathetic, but this is just a mask they frequently utilize to capture prey, like a spider in their web. Some of them, like Ted Bundy, look like the nice guy next door and do not have a threatening appearance or demeanor, but they are still monsters who will kill you without hesitation, so don't let them talk you into surrender.

Ted Bundy (Florida Department of Corrections)

In view of the above, a more important topic of discussion is to never give up the fight or stop thinking of how to escape. Hettinger gave up his gun, but still survived by having the initiative to run at the right time. Always remember what I stated about how much harder it is to hit a moving target than a stationary one, especially with a pistol. Even if you have been shot several times by the bad guys, do not give up. Your mind is your most powerful weapon. If you have convinced yourself you are going to die, you probably will. Never give up that will to fight, or to run, to survive. I have known narcotics agents who wrestled with suspects for their guns for over five minutes. Some of them had the hell beaten out of them in the process, but never let go of their weapons, and thereby survived. They were able to hold control of their weapons long enough for backup to arrive and rescue them. Never give up the fight to survive!

Never surrender your weapon!

Rule 12

Proper Distance

This is one of the most important rules for you to remember for your survival as an armed citizen, especially if you are the average female, small male, or elderly person. I know, I can hear all of you feminists out there screaming obscenities at me right now, but the reality, whether you like it or not, is that the average female does not have the upper body strength to defeat the average male in a physical confrontation. I have a black belt in Okinawan Goju-ryu karate and I do acknowledge there are some females, such as UFC professional fighters, who might be able to kick my tail in a physical fight, but this is not the norm for the female population.

If you have the drop on your adversary and you are pointing your gun at him and telling him to freeze, or telling him to drop his gun, why in the world would you move close to him where he could get an easy shot at you with a hidden weapon or possibly allow him to grab your firearm, if he is unarmed, and take it away from you? Stay behind cover if you can and tell him to immediately drop his weapon (gun, club, or knife) and put his hands in the air. If he does not immediately comply with this demand he probably has another agenda, his mind is racing to evaluate if he can intimidate you or get the drop on you. It may become prudent for you to shoot him if he does not immediately comply with your commands and you are in fear of your life. It only takes a split second for the suspect to raise his gun and shoot you. Keep your eyes on his hands. Remember that his hands are what will kill you.

Okay, if the suspect has now dropped his weapon and complied with your demands, have you thought about what you do now? Let him think that you are aggressive and crazy and will shoot him if he moves in your direction. Scream obscenities at him and let him think you are violent by nature, like he is, and actually want to shoot him if he doesn't do what you demand, "I will blow your head off if you even think about moving in my direction! Go ahead, just make my day!" Order him to lie down on the ground, put his hands behind his head and stay there until you tell him to move or you will "blow his head off"! Don't forget that he is a predator who will evaluate your demeanor to ascertain if you are weak and might hesitate to fire if he assaults you. If you show any weakness whatsoever, he will be much more likely to challenge or assault you, or to run. If someone else is with you, have them call the police while you maintain a sight picture on the criminal with both hands on your gun. If you are alone, use your cell phone in one hand to call 911 while you keep your strong hand and your eyes on your pistol pointed at the criminal. Keep your distance so you know you could easily shoot him, at least 21 feet away, before he could ever get a hand on your weapon. Don't attempt to tie him up. Just keep him on the ground until the police arrive. If he decides to disregard your commands, gets up and runs, then just let him run. But if he lunges at you after this type of encounter, you should be in fear of your life. Assume he is attempting to take your pistol away and shoot him.

The bottom line is to maintain proper distance to keep your weapon out of reach of your adversary. Distance is usually in your favor, especially if you are a small female confronting a large male suspect. Never forget that even 8% to 10% of the trained police officers killed in the line of duty were killed with their own guns when the unarmed suspects managed to wrestle their pistols away from them. Even if you are a very tough young man who is a college wrestler, has a black belt in karate, and has never lost a fight in your life, don't let your machismo take precedence over your common sense. This is not a macho fighting tournament, this is life and death survival, so why take any chances? Keep your gun pointed at him from a distance of at least 21 feet and call the police to come take custody and handcuff this violent criminal. That is what they are paid for, and they would actually prefer you let them do that.

The statistics on police officers killed in the line of duty support keeping distance between the officer and the suspects. You should keep this in mind if you are an armed civilian. The statistics show that officers tend to die in up close encounters. They are more frequently successful in apprehending their attackers and to survive unscathed as the distance increases. Distance buys time. Waiting buys time. Time buys survival.

As shown above, never let the suspect get this close to you! The weaver stance is great if you have distance between you and your adversary, but at ultra close range, if you use this type of stance, the suspect can easily grab your weapon before you get off a shot. Action is quicker than reaction. If the suspect lunges at you, be prepared to rapidly pull back your weapon and shoot from the hip as shown in the 3rd photograph above. It is prudent to practice some hip shooting for accuracy at ultra close distance in the event you are ever assaulted in this fashion and the suspect is trying to take your weapon away.

Rule 13

Reliability Of Weapons & Equipment

If you ever want to see the real man-eater lions of Tsavo, they are still on display in the Field Museum of Natural History in Chicago, Illinois.

Is your equipment reliable, tested, and well maintained? Never bring an untested weapon into battle! For civilians, this probably only means your firearm and possibly a flashlight and cell phone, but for police and the military it includes a wide variety of support equipment such as handcuffs, radios, flashlights, batons, tasers, etc. Having the battery go out on your flashlight in a dark building with a burglar, because you forgot to change the batteries, could become as dangerous as having your firearm jam during a gunfight. Aside from testing your firearms for reliability, it is also important to test the sights of your firearm for accuracy. Most firearms have adjustable sights. These sights might be right on target for the individual from whom you purchased or borrowed the firearm, but can be totally off base for your shooting eye. This is especially important if you are utilizing a rifle with a telescopic scope and you have not sighted in the weapon for your individual proper windage and elevation levels.

As a law enforcement officer, with over 27 years of experience, I could tell you about the countless times I have seen professional law enforcement officers fail to maintain or bring essential equipment with them to arrest situations. Fortunately, they always remember to bring their weapons, but I cannot tell you how many times I have seen federal agents and plain clothes police officers fail to remember to bring handcuffs, flashlights, and other essential equipment with them during arrest scenarios. Police detectives and federal agents frequently have to run back to their vehicles to obtain handcuffs, flashlights, and other essential equipment from their glove box or trunk of their car, which they should have brought with them during the initial course of the arrest. With uniformed police, this is rare, as they make arrests several times a day and display most of their equipment on their gun belts and tend to inspect each other during roll call. I am going to give you another Hollywood movie scenario to explain the importance of this rule. I do this to provide you with an example you can easily visualize and remember if you have seen this frequently viewed film.

I have hunted extremely dangerous game in Africa (Cape Buffalo), and I am going to tell you the story about the greatest hunt of predators in human history, but these predators were not people, but lions. The lions known as the Ghost and the Darkness were unlike any other lions previously observed. Man-eaters as a rule are rare, but these lions seemed to kill for the actual pleasure of it - something unheard of and never before documented. They were like human serial killers. Their bloody killing spree spread terror through the countryside and the railroad worker camps at Tsavo in Africa, effectively halting the plans of railroad expansion of the greatest colonial empire on earth at the time, the British Empire. The local natives believed these lions were spirits, demons, and the engineer in charge of building a railroad through their hunting grounds, knew they had to be stopped. For 9 months in 1898, these two lions terrorized the southern Kenyan region of Tsavo, killing as many as **135** people by one account. It was the chronicle of the hunt for these lions by Colonel Patterson that became one of the most thrilling true stories ever told and was the basis for the movie *The Ghost and the Darkness*. So how accurate was the Hollywood depiction of this incredible story and what does it have to do with this rule of survival?

Colonel Patterson was the British engineer tasked to build the 100-yard bridge over the Tsavo River. As if geographic challenges were not enough to defeat most faced with this task, a pair of lions proceeded to complicate matters by killing many of his railroad workers. Patterson had only been at Tsavo for a matter of days when he received reports about workers disappearing. Although he was told that lions were responsible, Patterson did not believe these accounts at first. Upon investigation, it was learned that not one but two lions were indeed responsible for the carnage. Early attempts to hunt down and kill the lions were unsuccessful. Patterson would write in his book that the lions seemed to be able to predict what he would do next. What we do not see clearly in the film is the fact that there were many camps scattered up and down the railway for over 30 miles. Thus these lions could attack different camps each time making it impossible to predict where they would strike next. However, the frustration and fear felt by Patterson and the workers is most effectively conveyed in the movie. In his memoirs Patterson wrote, *"(The lions) methods became so uncanny, and their man-stalking so well-timed and so certain of success, that the workmen firmly believed they were not real animals at all, but devils in lions' shape."*

The movie may have exaggerated some of the more terrifying acts of these lions in order to make a more interesting film, but reality itself was not too different. In the film, Patterson makes the serious mistake of letting the camp Doctor talk him into exchanging rifles before hunting the lions. The Doctor advised Patterson that his rifle was a higher caliber that was more powerful than Patterson's rifle and was therefore more prudent to utilize. Unbelievably, Patterson never test fired the Doctor's rifle before he ventured out into the bush to hunt the lions. There is a terrifying scene in the film where Patterson is facing one of the lions, has the lion in his sights, but click, the borrowed rifle misfired and Patterson was extremely lucky the lion just ran away and didn't eat him. This is the most important point I hope you remember from this story. **Never bring an untested weapon into battle!** I know what many gun owners are thinking when they read this story, "I can't believe Patterson would bring a rifle he never shot to hunt two lions which have killed over 100 people. I would never make that type of mistake!" I ask you, if you had a home invasion right now and that "lion" violent criminal was threatening your family, how many of you would pick up a firearm from the closet you haven't inspected, shot, or cleaned in over 10 years? How many of you would pick up that new pistol you just recently purchased at the gun store, but never yet test fired on the range? With over 27 years of law enforcement experience, I have heard the stories of the empty gun that was assumed to be loaded, the sidearm so neglected it failed to fire, or how the old or dirty ammo (green with verdigris) failed to fire.

And yes, Patterson's rifle did misfire in real life, and it was nearly as dramatic a moment as depicted in the film though there was not a professional hunter named Remington or Masai warriors to back him up in the real story. Patterson was a brave man who learned from his mistakes and returned to the bush to eventually kill both the lions. And like the movie, the end of this incredible story was a very happy one - the workers returned, the bridge was built, and the railhead was soon to reach Nairobi. On January 30th, 1899, the workers presented a silver bowl to Patterson in appreciation for the bravery he had shown in relentlessly hunting down the man-eaters. I hope the advice provided in this book will help you to enjoy the same success, whether you are shooting violent predators called lions, or forced to shoot violent human predators.

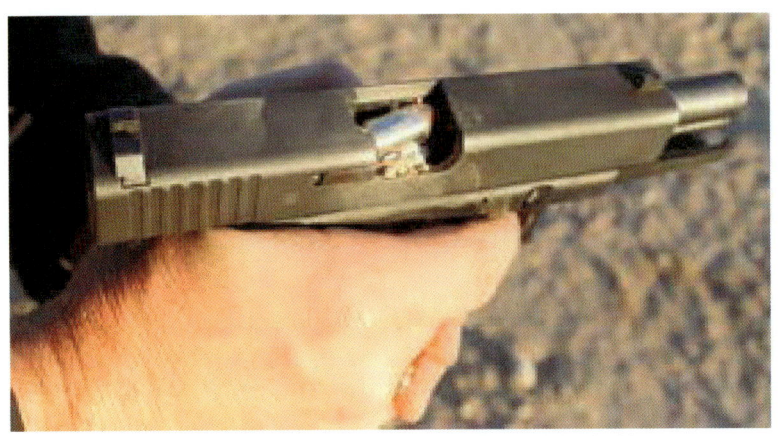

Is your weapon and ammunition clean and reliable?

Rule 14

Handgun And Caliber Selection

One of the most controversial topics among gun owners and firearms instructors is what type and caliber of handgun you should carry for self-defense. The opinions are as numerous as the huge selection of handguns you have to choose from. Even the expert law enforcement trainers and firearms instructors from numerous federal, state, and local police departments disagree, and this is why we see so many different types and calibers of handguns issued to different police departments across the country. There are hundreds of articles about this subject you can read on the internet and in gun magazines, so you can research those sources if you have a high interest. I am not going to burden you with what would be an extremely long essay about the strengths and weaknesses of every type and caliber of handgun. I will give you my opinion and some general guidelines on what you should consider, based on your experience with handguns, how much you plan to train with that handgun in the future, and how sensitive you are to a flinch reaction (remember RULE #7).

Once again, I am going to tell you a short story to hopefully explain why I give you the advice contained in this rule. When I was a young rookie police officer in Dallas, Texas, way back in 1979, I was put on the night shift patrolling the Central Patrol Division and was temporarily assigned to an older veteran partner named "Johnnie". Johnnie was a very big man who weighed over 280 pounds and was a good police officer who had made numerous arrests. I stepped into our marked police car to start our 12 am. to 8 am. shift and one of the first questions the old veteran asked me was "What kind of gun are you carrying son?" I replied that I carried a Smith & Wesson .357 magnum caliber revolver (very few police officers carried semi-auto pistols back then, a topic I will discuss more later). Johnnie then asked me what type of scores I had with the Dallas Police Pistol Qualification course and I replied I had a 99% score on the most recent qualification. Johnnie then stated, "Son, with a score like that you should carry a real man's gun. You should get rid of that pea shooter and get a S&W .44 magnum caliber pistol with a 6 inch barrel like I carry. This will knock them down. Your gun will just piss them off." It is noted Johnnie's gun is the same handgun carried by "Dirty Harry" in all the Hollywood movies. I played the submissive rookie and wisely did not question his wisdom.

About a year later, I found out that Johnnie got into his first shooting incident. Johnnie was reportedly facing a violent burglar who resisted and evaded arrest. The burglar was only about 5 yards in front of Johnnie when Johnnie fired his .44 magnum caliber revolver at the suspect, but Johnnie missed with all 6 rounds and the suspect ran and escaped apprehension. If I remember correctly, you have to score at least 70% in Dallas Police qualification courses (targets at 7, 15, & 25 yards) with your pistol in order to be allowed to carry the weapon, so something went terribly wrong for Johnnie that night. I don't know if it was stress or the recoil from this heavy caliber pistol that destroyed Johnnie's marksmanship that night, but I think he might have been better off with a .22 caliber pistol with almost no recoil, than Dirty Harry's weapon of choice that night. Johnnie was a very self confident officer who had seen a lot of action, so I believe it was more likely flinch from recoil, than stress, which killed his accuracy.

The bottom line is that the .44 magnum revolver and the .45, .40, and .357 Sig caliber semi-automatic pistols will probably have better stopping power than a .22, .25, .32, or .380 small caliber pistol, but if the large calibers cause you to flinch and miss your target you might be better off with a smaller caliber pistol. The bottom line is, the caliber of your pistol is not as important as your accuracy with the weapon. A .22 caliber round which hits your adversary between the eyes is much better than a .44 magnum caliber round that missed him. Pick the caliber and handgun you can be accurate with. Don't get me wrong, if you are an excellent marksman who can handle the heavier recoil and still have great accuracy, I have no doubt you are better off with a .44, .45, or .40 caliber pistol which has much better stopping power. New or infrequent shooters might not have that ability to be accurate with a high caliber handgun—so don't automatically tell them they must get those high caliber handguns to protect themselves unless you know they plan to dedicate the practice time and effort to become very accurate shots with them. Sometimes, even people like Johnnie who qualify with a handgun at least twice a year, and have fairly good range scores, miss their targets at close range when the handgun they are shooting is "the most powerful handgun known to man". It is noted that even higher .50 caliber Desert Eagle handguns are now available for purchase to the general public.

Semi-automatic Pistol Or Revolver?

When I first became a Dallas police officer back in 1978, I heard many old timers state, "Six shots for sure is better than 15 shots maybe!" They also commented that revolvers are very simple to operate, you don't need to worry about a safety, and they are less likely to malfunction. You don't need to worry about how to clear a stove top jam or many of the other possible malfunctions of a semi-auto pistol with a revolver. While the military certainly had a need for high capacity magazines with the multiple adversaries they would face in battle, it was argued that simplicity and reliability were far more important for police officers who only face one or two adversaries at close range in the vast majority of deadly force situations. I think there was great wisdom in this, but technology has changed since those days and the new top of the line, off the shelf semi-automatic pistols, are generally much more reliable than they used to be back in 1978. I do not want to mention manufacturers names, but I do know that many of those older model semi-auto pistols, especially those in .25, .32, .380, and 9mm caliber, frequently jammed when I experimented with them back in the 1970's and 1980's. I would be remiss if I didn't point out that the classic Colt 1911 model .45 caliber semi-auto pistol is an exception, a different story and a legendary man stopper, as proven in the conflict in the Philippine War of Insurrection. Even some of the quality older Colt .45 caliber semi- autos can jam, but if you have a good gunsmith who knows how to tune up your pistol correctly, this shouldn't be a problem to correct. Like any quality work, it might cost you some money to insure reliability.

When I was hired as a CIA Special Agent in 1982 and attended the CIA Office of Security weapons training, I observed that the CIA was also still training with revolvers and issued revolvers to special agents of the Office of Security such as myself. Back in those days, the revolvers were used for dignitary protection details for KGB defectors and the CIA Director William Casey. I am sure they have probably switched to semi-automatic pistols and even more sophisticated tactical weapons by now, but who knows as everything is classified with the CIA.

When I transferred from CIA to become a DEA Special Agent in 1985 (believe it or not, but the DEA actually pays its agents 25% more in availability pay than the CIA), I was also trained with a Smith & Wesson .357 magnum revolver. I was in one of the first basic agent classes of DEA in 1985 to be trained at the new DEA Academy which was now co-located with the FBI Academy in Quantico, Virginia, and we shared the same firearms ranges with the FBI. Both the FBI and DEA were still using revolvers at that time.

Only a couple years after my DEA Academy graduation, I believe DEA became the first major federal law enforcement agency to issue semi-automatic pistols to their special agents. At first they issued only Glock and Sig-Sauer 9 mm pistols. They only wanted to issue double action pistols, not single action like the old Colt .45, because of the issue of remembering to cock the hammer in preparation for action and/or take off the safety that I have already mentioned. Extensive testing was conducted by the DEA firearms staff to verify the reliability of these two pistols before they were approved. After they were approved and the FBI firearms instructors saw the DEA agents shooting them for qualifications on the neighboring ranges at the FBI Academy, some of the FBI firearms instructors reportedly established a semi- surveillance of the DEA agents shooting the new Glock and Sig- Sauer pistols on the range. The FBI was reportedly keeping track of the number of firearms malfunctions and "jams" to ascertain the reliability of this new generation of semi-auto pistols.

The new semi-auto pistols proved to be very reliable, evidently as reliable as revolvers, and passed the test as reliable for the FBI, as the DEA had already ascertained. A couple years later the FBI followed suit with the DEA and approved their agents to carry semi-auto pistols like the DEA agents. Around 1990, the DEA upgraded again and began to issue .40 caliber Glock and Sig-Sauer pistols to their agents. DEA agents were also allowed to carry the U.S. military approved Beretta 9mm or their own personally owned single action .45 caliber semi-auto and several other types of handguns, if they could qualify on the range with them, but only double action pistols were issued to new agents. In view of the fact DEA agents frequently participate in undercover assignments, I feel they were very prudent in allowing this flexibility in weapon choice. It would not be a good thing for drug traffickers to know that DEA undercover agents only carried one specific type of handgun; unbelievably, this is the case with some other law enforcement agencies who only issue one weapon option to their undercover operatives.

In 1986, after the FBI had the Miami shootout that resulted in the death of 2 special agents and the wounding of 5 other special agents, the FBI decided to re-evaluate their selection of handguns to be issued to new agents and decided to allow more powerful handguns. Instead of permitting their agents the option to switch to the .45 caliber round (if they could handle the recoil), which the DEA had already found to be reliable and have better stopping power than the 9mm, the FBI decided to utilize the 10mm round and develop a special pistol, just for the FBI. This would, in theory, be superior to the pistol utilized by any other law enforcement agency. It turned out this 10mm pistol specially developed for the FBI was a failure as the recoil was much too severe for the female agents and your average male agent to have the ability to maintain good accuracy.

The FBI eventually switched back to the same type of .40 caliber pistols being carried by the DEA, for issue to new FBI agents. Why they did not just immediately switch to the .45 or .40 caliber pistol, which were already proven man-stoppers with a higher relative incapacitation index than the 9mm, is beyond my understanding. *The bottom line lesson of this rule is to remember that if something already works well, don't try to fix it!* I have no problem with research and evaluation to attempt to develop something better, but don't just get a new gun to start something new so that you appear different, special, or look more macho on the range. We all want to be special, but go with something that is prudent and proven before you attempt to be special. Just like Colonel Patterson in the previous rule, if you know the rifle you have already works well, don't switch to an unproven rifle in a life and death situation just because it is new and they tell you it is more powerful. If you do, you might get eaten by the lions.

From left to right-A .40 caliber hollow point bullet vs a .40 caliber full metal jacket bullet.

Regardless of your handgun and caliber selection, keep in mind that the type of ammunition you select can also be very important. Hollow point bullets in a pistol will generally have better stopping power than a full metal jacket bullet. For self-defense, hollow point bullets are the way to go. They feature an exaggerated opening at the front of the bullet. The idea is that this opening will force the projectile to expand upon impact, dumping all of the energy to create a massive wound. Another reason hollow point bullets are the bullet of choice for police is because when they hit something they expand and are less likely to go through the suspect and injure people behind him. I have read recent news reports that the FBI is now re-evaluating again and considering re- adopting the 9mm semi-auto pistol because of recent improvements to 9mm Luger ammunition.

On July 25, 2014, the FBI released a pre-solicitation notice for a family of pistols chambered in 9mm and in doing so has started the great debate about .45 and/or .40 caliber versus 9mm again. Defenders of this movement are quoted as follows: "It's not that the .40 S&W failed to deliver the terminal performance they wanted. It's just that the new breed of 9mm ammunition can deliver similar performance without the generally snappier recoil and accelerated wear (on both pistol and shooter), at a more affordable price. The fact the new pistols can house more of the cartridges in the same sized gun is an added bonus." The FBI reported the majority of FBI shooters are both faster and more accurate with shooting a 9mm Luger than shooting a .40 S&W (similar sized weapon). The FBI is very conservative and has an excellent testing facility for this new generation of 9mm Luger ammunition, so I would put much credibility in their studies. I have always been a fan of the .40 and .45 calibers, but if this new 9mm Luger ammunition truly has essentially the same terminal performance as the .40 and .45 calibers, but allows better accuracy for the average shooter, they may be very prudent in making this change. Only time will tell.

Based on the above, when you ask me what type of handgun you should utilize for self- defense, the answer from my experience perspective is relatively simple. I am not going to be a pimp for any firearms manufacturer and say this is the only weapon or caliber you should carry! I also do not claim to be the total expert on firearms or self-defense just because I shot at more than one bad guy during my career. Go to the firearms range and test several types of handguns to determine for yourself which handgun is the most reliable and accurate for you as an individual. We are all a little different in capabilities, but if you do not plan to practice shooting on a regular basis I recommend you are probably better off with a .410 caliber Taurus Judge or Smith & Wesson Governor revolver for home protection. It is noted these two revolvers are illegal in California. I assume California law considers them to be similar to a sawed-off shotgun in view of the short barrel. These pistols allow you the advantage of having a mini shotgun in a pistol size package and offer a wide variety of types of .410 shotgun shells you can utilize in this pistol. I like the Winchester PDX1 Defender loads which have 3 plated disc projectiles as well as 12 plated BBs in each shell. Remember that the vast majority of police and armed citizen shootings take place at very close range. This type of handgun, when loaded with the shotgun shells, is not good for long range shots; but the inexperienced shooter will have a much better chance of hitting the target at close range with this mini shotgun spray (3 large & 12 small projectiles) each time you pull the trigger, especially if it is a moving target you are firing at.

If you can handle recoil, and practice target shooting on a regular basis, you are not an inexperienced shooter, and should probably get a quality .45, .40, or .357 Sig semi-automatic, or perhaps even a high dollar U.S.P.S.A. style modified .38 super (a gunsmith tricked out semi-auto pistol), as you probably know how to clear an unlikely, but possible, semi-auto malfunction quickly. I own a Sig-Sauer and a Glock .40 caliber semi-auto with tritium night sights and I frequently target shoot with them on my ranch in Arizona. I sometimes have to shoot coyotes on the ranch, who attempt to eat my wife's chickens, with a very accurate and reliable Bushmaster AR-15 carbine equipped with a night vision sight. I also have a Remington

1100 semi-auto shotgun with 00 buck shells for home protection at close ranges. That shotgun also works extremely well for shooting the rattlesnakes that frequently come near our livestock. I don't think of myself as a survivalist, but just as a retired federal agent who is prepared for the bad guys and the animal predators. My wife doesn't like guns much and does not target shoot, so she has a .410 caliber Taurus Judge which also works well for her to shoot the rattlesnakes if I am gone. The 12-gauge shotgun has too much kick for her to shoot comfortably.

If you want to become a true handgun expert, I strongly recommend you attend one of the basic NRA firearms courses, or United States Concealed Carry Association (U.S.C.C.A.) courses, then practice to the point that you are capable of participating in the very professional United States Practical Shooting Association (U.S.P.S.A.) competition shooting matches. These competition matches involve true combat shooting type experiences that are judged on a combination of speed, as well as accuracy. This is not just target shooting at stationary targets. You will shoot on the run, from behind barricades, and at moving targets. You will perform mandatory magazine changes while running between barricades. They test a variety of your skills and ability to reload rapidly, or shoot with your weak hand on certain stages of the courses. I have participated in these competition shooting matches. I hate to admit it, but these U.S.P.S.A. competition shooters are much better combat handgun shooters than the vast majority of police officers and soldiers. Keep in mind these guys are professionals and real "barrel suckers" who spend hundreds of hours practicing their skill every year, so don't be disappointed if you don't do well at first. Practice makes perfect. Many of them are sponsored by firearms manufacturers and have high quality $5,000 pistols which have been fine tuned by the best gunsmiths in the nation. If you want to become highly proficient with your handgun, then join the U.S.P.S.A. and participate in a few of these matches. You will be amazed how much you will learn and quickly realize how limited your skills were before you participated.

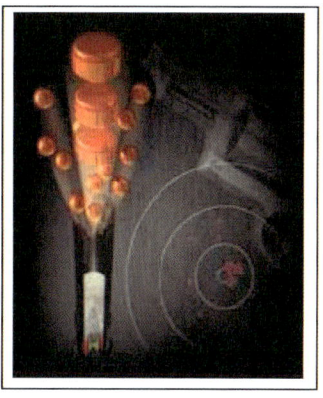

The Winchester PDX1 .410 shotshell was developed specifically for the Taurus Judge line of revolvers. It consists of a shot cup with 12 BBs and 3 plated disks. The thinking is that the disks tend to stay together due to their profile, as opposed to buckshot that is round and forces the balls apart quicker in the pattern. The 12 BBs are meant as additional insurance that something hits your target.

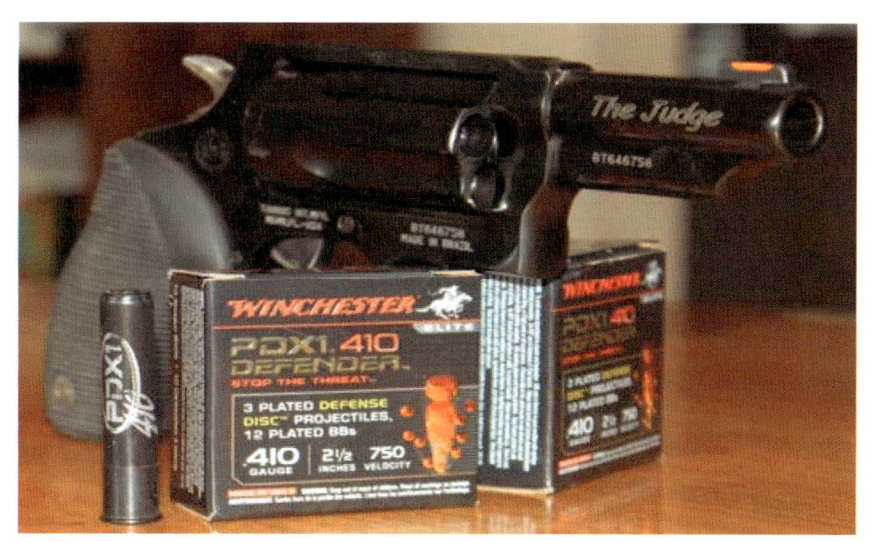

Highly effective in both shotguns and 410 compatible handguns, the PDX1 in 410 gauge features a distinctive black hull and black oxide high-base head and combines three plated Defense Disc™ projectiles and 12 pellets of plated BB shot. The result is the ideal personal protection load for short range engagement with the performance needed to stop threats. This load is also suitable for varmint hunting and pest control. Designed for use in the Taurus Judge, this new personal defense round provides maximum protection at close range.

Rule 15

Proper Holster Selection

Brad Kozak, former editor with TheTruthAboutGuns.com wrote an excellent article about holster selection in which he stated, "Hollywood has created the myth that all the cowboys in the Old West carried their guns on their hips in low slung thigh holsters. In reality, many of these type of holsters were invented by stuntmen looking for a fast way to enable actors to draw their pistols and fire with a quick draw for the camera. These type of holsters do enable a quick draw, but keep in mind they also enable your adversaries to more easily draw it for you and shoot you with it. The paradox in holster selection is that the holster which enables a fast draw is usually less secured for someone to take it away from you, but if you do get a highly secure holster it is not easy to draw and you might not get the first shot." Pictured above is a full flap holster with a sewn on extra magazine pouch. This type of holster provides fairly good security and protection from the elements, but certainly does not facilitate a super fast draw.

My preference in holsters for those who open carry would be a tactical retention holster similar to the Ghost III holster (pictured top of page 94). This type of holster features a locking system, modular design and rotatable belt attachment. The weapon draw is instinctive and very quick for the natural movement of the hand. Holsters which provide a locking system, or some type of thumb break or secret release mechanism, provide added security for police officers to prevent the handgun from being easily snatched away from them!

Kozak further stated, "Some armed citizens choose to 'open carry' their pistols. In my opinion, that is fine if you are out hunting in the forest, a police officer in uniform, or a soldier on the battlefield, but if you open carry in a bad part of town you are probably just asking for trouble. If you have a concealed carry permit, I see little advantage to 'open carry'. Most armed citizens are prudent and trouble aversive and realize that discretion is the better part of valor." I agree with Kozak and it is my opinion that "open carry" might enable you to draw a second quicker, but you are giving up the element of surprise to get the drop on an adversary who didn't know you were armed. The brilliant tactician Niccolò Machiavelli once stated, "No enterprise for the enemy is more likely to succeed than one which is concealed until ripe for execution!"

Ghost III holster
Triple K
www.triplek.com

The Pocket Pistol

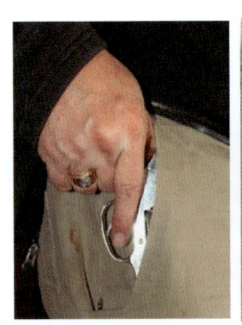

Even the armed citizen who does not have a concealed carry permit and is not planning to take their handgun out of the house or car should give some consideration to obtaining a holster for their pistol. Not all home invasions involve a dramatic warning by the noise of kicking in the front door of your residence. A significant number of home invasions involve suspects who scam entrance to your home under such false pretenses as a door to door salesman, pretend an introduction as a friend of your teenage daughter, etc., or with false pretenses such as "I just had a car accident down the street, can I please use your phone to call for help?" A gun locked up in a bedroom or safe will probably do you no good if the suspect has already gained entrance to your home. Believe it or not, a pocket can be a good place to carry a gun, if you have the right kind of gun. A hammerless wheelgun or a small semi-auto, without sharp edges to prevent a snag, will fit nicely into your pocket if you wear pants with large pockets, or cargo pocket style pants. Some manufacturers make pocket holsters that will hold a small frame handgun and utilize fabrics that grip on the outside, but are smooth on the inside, so the holster will stay in your pocket when you draw the gun.

DeSantis Cargo Pocket holster www.desantisholster.com

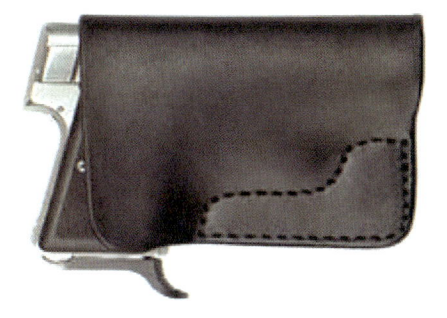

Pictured above is the "Urban Defender" pocket holster for small semi- automatics. Designed to be carried in your front or hip pocket for maximum concealment. www.TripleK.com

The Wallet Gun

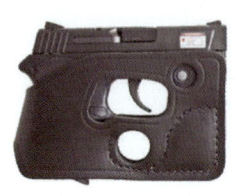

Pictured left is the DeSantis "Pocket Shot" wallet holster.

You might also consider always carrying a wallet holster which usually only works to carry a small caliber semi-automatic handgun or a derringer, but is certainly better than not having access to any weapon during a surprise deadly force assault. Most of us will not carry a large caliber handgun 24/7 because of the discomfort and inconvenience involved, but might consider carrying a pocket pistol or wallet gun 24/7 in view of the light weight, convenience, comfort, and ready access. The concealed carry of a small caliber pistol, like the wallet guns pictured above, makes a good backup weapon and is certainly better than having no weapon available in a surprise assault.

The Shoulder Holster

When I was attending the Dallas Police Academy, I remember the advice an older officer told us during an Officer Survival Training Program. He stated, "I know that at least half of you are going to go out and buy shoulder holsters after you graduate, that is fine, but believe me you will rarely wear them after the first year of purchase. We all grew up watching Elliot Ness and the Untouchables along with other gangster movies, and thought how cool that looked to wear a shoulder holster. But in reality, you will probably only utilize that shoulder holster two or three times a year when you wear a suit." He was right, I wanted to "look cool" and purchased a shoulder holster and have worn that shoulder holster maybe a total of ten times in the last 35 years! Why is that? The reason is because you can't take your coat off in public without telling the world you are carrying a handgun. For the concealed carry permit holder, this means you can't take your coat off in most states! So what do you do? When you enter a hot environment, do you just sit and sweat because you can't take off your jacket? Well, I guess that isn't really cool after all. I know they look cool, but think about it before you waste the money.

With a holster that is on your hip, you can take your jacket off, preferably when no one is watching, and then carefully drape your jacket across your hip holster for concealment when you sit down at a restaurant.

A shoulder holster does have great practicality if you are a U.S. Army soldier in a tank. They are also great to carry a large handgun for hunting in the bush, under a loose fitting jacket, as it protects the pistol from the elements, but I don't think you will find this type of holster practical for daily carry in an urban environment unless you live in a very cold climate which would make no one question the fact you are always wearing a coat or jacket.

Innovative Shoulder Holster Alternative

UnderTech UnderCover introduces the new Coolux Mesh shirts (top left photo on page 98) that breathe and wick moisture away from the body. The exclusive Coolux Mesh fabric fits like a second skin and enables you to carry and conceal a full-sized handgun. It's modeled after their extremely popular compression shirts that are considered to be one of the most comfortable methods to carry a self-defense handgun. The holster is designed to carry and conceal just about any self-defense handgun (right hand draw only), while the travel pockets are perfect for concealing and carrying valuable items such as your passport, credit cards, cash, cell phone, etc. in the zippered pockets.

The Hip Holster

In the author's opinion, the hip holster is probably the most practical selection for a police officer or armed citizen who wishes to carry a large caliber handgun on his person. Hip holsters are holsters positioned on your side, or in the small of your back, or the front of your waistband. They can be carried on the inside or outside of the waistband and allow a fairly rapid draw while also affording fairly good concealment from the general public. Carrying the gun on the outside of the waistband requires that you wear a shirt or jacket to cover the weapon. There are numerous designs and they come in a variety of different "cants" (the angle in which the gun is held).

The Amadini paddle holster (pictured above), is much preferred by police officers because it is easy to slip on and off your belt, thereby avoiding the hassle of having to unbuckle your belt and slide the holster through the belt and your belt loops every time you remove or put on your holster.

The Triple Threat holster allows the option to carry your gun in three positions, strong side, cross draw, or behind the back.

The carry of a handgun on the inside of the waistband is preferred by many armed citizens. It works well, unless you have a beer gut. In that case, you will find that your love handles cover the grip of your gun and make it difficult to remove from the holster. If you are relatively thin, the inside the waistband holsters work great. I could write a hundred pages about the different types of holsters, but the bottom line is that most people will wear or carry what is comfortable to them. If your holster is not comfortable, you will only wear it for a short period of time and then leave it at home, with your handgun, when it is most needed. Murphy's Law is that the one time you leave your gun at home is when you need it — so get a holster which is comfortable and works for you. A holster which you carry every day, so that you have that firearm when you need it!

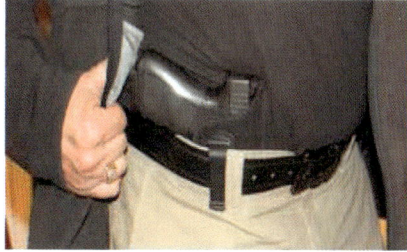

Outside and inside Waistband Hip Holster

Another Waistband Carrying Option

The "Belly Band" is one of the most versatile and comfortable methods of concealment available. You can wear it in almost every situation! Whether you dress up for the office or go to the gym, the Belly Band can be there, totally concealed and ready! It's made in the USA of heavy duty elastic with a Velcro closure. It has two ambidextrous slots: one for an automatic pistol and one for a revolver. It has a 6-inch pocket which conceals important papers, cash, credit cards, as well as a slot for a spare magazine. It works great with medium and small frame revolvers and semi-automatic pistols. It is pictured with a Glock 19 and will easily accommodate a full sized Glock 17, 22 even the Glock 21 & all the mini Glocks. It will even work with all of the popular self-defense handguns including 1911, SIGs and Beretta. With the Belly Band you can discreetly and comfortably conceal your handguns under a variety of shirts and sweaters.

Pictured (left) is a ladies leather pistol purse. The pistol pocket is closed with Velcro. It features a zippered inside pocket and a large outside pocket secured with a magnetic snap for extra security.

Best Woman Holster

The best holster for a woman may not be a holster, but a handbag. A purse can easily hide the "imprint" of a concealed weapon even better than a shirt covering a waistband holster. Almost all women carry a purse of some type and there are many manufacturers for purses that have specialized holsters contained within the purse to hide a concealed handgun. If you have a focus for fashion, there are numerous styles and even fashion designs of gun compatible handbags for you to choose from. The handbag holster also offers one additional benefit that the common street thug would never anticipate. You can shoot through the handbag to hit the unsuspecting, would be rapist or mugger, without ever even showing you have a gun!

The Bra Holster

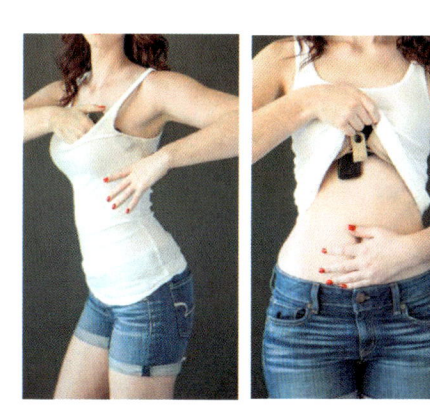

In view of the fact the first item a purse-snatcher or thief would likely target during a robbery would be the woman's purse, many women prefer not to carry their handgun in their purse. One holster option to consider, for ladies who don't like to carry their handgun in their purse or wear baggy clothing to cover the imprint of a large handgun holster, is the "Flashbang" modified push up bra holster pictured above left. Another option is the "Marilyn" model holster pictured above right. Some female police officers also choose this type of holster for their back-up handgun. Both these holsters types and many others are available.

The Flashbang bra holster comes with three straps of different lengths to accommodate the majority of bras. Each strap has a directional snap that allows you to quickly put the holster on and take it off. Because the gun actually rests partially inside the bra cup, the only portion that's visible is the grip. Different strap sizes are included and the straps can be easily changed using a Phillips head screwdriver. Whether or not this type of holster works for you or your body composition or size, is of course a personal decision.

The Ankle Holster

Left: DeSantis Apache Ankle Rig
Right: DeSantis Leather Ankle Holster

When I was a Dallas police officer, I carried an ankle holster with a .38 caliber snub nose revolver for a very short period of time as a back-up weapon, until I was involved in my first foot chase while carrying that ankle holster. This foot chase was the only foot chase I ever lost in my four years of service with the DPD, and also the last time I every carried an ankle holster. The idea of an ankle holster as a back-up weapon appears reasonable, until you realize this type of holster is going to beat the hell out of your ankle if you ever get into a high-speed foot pursuit. I am not a fan of the ankle holster as a back-up weapon unless you don't ever plan to engage in a foot pursuit during an arrest. In addition, you have to bend over or raise a leg, putting you off balance or in a bad position, to confront your adversary and reach your weapon.

The Triple K Brand holster pictured above is designed to be worn on the ankle inside the trouser leg for maximum concealment. This holster is wet molded into a compact shape and equipped with a quick release thumb break safety strap. The shearling padded ankle band is made with an adjustable strap with Velcro®.

Tactical Open Carry Retention Holsters

REMINDER: As mentioned earlier, I do not recommend open carry of your firearm if you are an armed citizen with a concealed carry permit (CCP). Why let the criminal know you are armed and lose the element of surprise if you are assaulted? Police officers and the military are usually in uniform and thereby have no element of-surprise to lose via open carry. If you are going to open carry your firearm, I strongly advise you obtain a tactical retention holster similar to the DeSantis "Safety Star" pictured above. **Holsters that provide a locking system, or some type of thumb break or secret release mechanism, provide added security to prevent the handgun from being easily snatched away from you!**

Bottom Line on Holster Selection

Similar to my advice on handgun selection in the previous rule, don't pick a pistol just because it looks cool or you are told it is the most powerful. Just as you select a pistol based on good stopping power, but more important, you know you can shoot the most accurately; select a holster based on comfort and practicality. It doesn't really matter how it looks, the question is whether you will wear it every day. There is no limit to holster makers' inventiveness. There are numerous types of gun vests, pouches, and holsters. Most gun owners have a drawer full of holsters at home they will never wear again. Find your ideal holster. If you are not comfortable with your holster, keep looking until you find the right one you will wear every day. If you are not comfortable, you will not wear your gun. A gun that is left at home may be as useless as having no gun at all!

Rule 16

Never Assume Anything

"The lion cannot protect himself from traps, and the fox cannot defend himself from wolves. One must therefore be a fox to recognize traps, and a lion to frighten wolves."—Niccolò Machiavelli, The Prince

Never assume your adversary is unarmed and does not have back-up or hidden weapons! Even if the suspect is handcuffed he can still pose a significant threat, especially if he is a kick boxer or mixed martial artist. Always handcuff suspects with their hands behind their back or those handcuffs could be used to garrote you! Those of you who have seen the film *No Country for Old Men* certainly remember the dramatic scene where the suspect sneaks up behind the Sheriff's deputy and uses the handcuff chain to garrote him. Always keep an eye on your prisoner. Never trust the search of a fellow police officer and always conduct a thorough search yourself of every suspect taken into your custody. Police officers and military personnel have been killed by trusting a previous search, as the prisoner pulled a hidden weapon not discovered. During the long years of their prison incarceration, criminals have an endless supply of time to dream up weapons, tactics, scams, concealment and physical assault techniques to get the drop on you. **Some of them are wolves, and some are foxes, but they are all predators, so look for those traps they prepare for you.** Prisons are frequently an advanced training school for violent criminals. They are working out in the gym every day and exchanging devious ideas with other criminals while you are putting in your time in your 9 to 5 job every day. The following photographs are just a few examples why you should **NEVER ASSUME ANYTHING!**

Hidden Compartment

From left to right: Headrest that opens like a glove box to hide a pistol and a sawed off rifle hidden in vehicle center console.

Video Camera

Officers located a full size "Sharp" personal video recorder on the right rear passenger seat of a suspect's vehicle. Upon closer examination of the video camera, officers were able to remove a fake videocassette, which had been placed into the video camera. Once the videotape was removed, officers discovered a fully loaded "Taurus" 9mm.

Vending Machine

Officers of the Riley County Police Department executed a narcotics warrant in Manhattan, Kansas. During the search, officers located a Pepsi Machine converted into a gun safe that contained 17 firearms and more than 4,000 rounds of ammunition.

Billed Cap

(Provided by the 569th U.S. Forces Police)

This hat is made by Hawaiian Island Creations and is sold around the world. Usually has the pictured logo. Inside the hat, the front of the sweatband detaches with Velcro and the entire inside of the hat is a compartment. The discovering officer tested the hat and effectively concealed a .25 Beretta semi- auto pistol inside it.

Pen Knife and Gun

These pens hide a very sharp 2.25 inch knife blade made of 440A stainless steel. This is a slim-design knife pen which helps to disguise its dual purpose. Photo courtesy of www.smkw.com.

The Gun Storage Clock

Hairbrush Knife

An example of a knife made of plastic material and concealed as a hairbrush. The knife would not be able to be detected when going through a metal detector since its materials are composed of either porcelain or Kevlar. Photo courtesy of www.smkw.com.

The Cellphone Gun

The Italian Police uncovered a cellphone gun in a raid on the Italian Mafia.

Umbrella Sword

The Umbrella Sword-Most police officers suspect walking cane swords, but they now also sell umbrella swords. Photos courtesy of www.smkw.com.

Book Safe

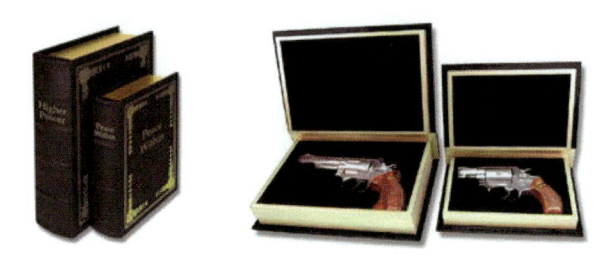

This book safe is cleverly designed and has been updated to look exactly like an ordinary book — which it is, until they hollowed out a secret compartment. This book diversion safe is perfect for hiding cash, jewelry, small guns or anything else you may want to conceal. And since these are real books with varying titles, they remain inconspicuous.

Belt Buckle And Bullet Shell Knives

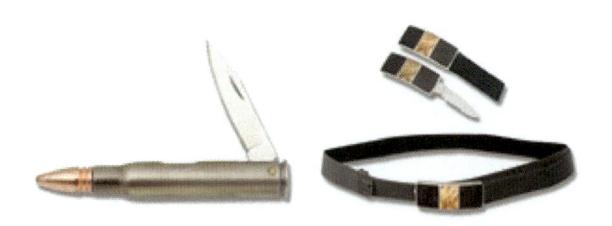

Zap Walking Cane Stun Gun

This ZAP Stun Walking Cane measures 32 inches and can be easily extended to 36 inches to accommodate users of different height. When threatened, the manufacture claims you can deliver a shocking 1 million volts of electric power that will cause your attacker's muscles to lose control, effectively immobilizing him for 5-10 minutes. Having a length of 32 to 36 inches also means that you can defend against your assailant, or aggressive dogs, from a safe distance away. This stun cane also comes with a built-in rechargeable battery and a flashlight in the handle. Photos courtesy of www.psproducts.com.

Fashion Pen and Lipstick Pepperspray

Pink fashion pen and false lipstick container which are actually pepper spray devices. Photos courtesy of www.smkw.com.

Self Defense Water Bottle

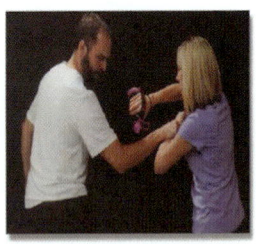

Browning® Black Label AquaForce Self Defense Water Bottle and Knife Combo. For the first time ever your water bottle offers more than a refreshing pause when out jogging or around town. The patent pending design becomes an excellent self-defense tool should the need arrive.

Under Desk Concealment Plate with Holster

This is one of those "cool" items you'd think you only see in the movies… but it actually has true functionality and lots of real world uses! www.undertechundercover.com markets an aluminum plate that accepts a Blackhawk Serpa-Lock Holster (included). The holster attaches to the plate using the same screws that come with the holster. The plate has four mounting holes drilled into the four corners that allow you to mount the plate and holster under your desk, counter, table, etcetera, wherever you need access to a handgun quickly. It's perfect for executives at work and storeowners.

Globe Gun Safe and Concealment Cans

Cellphone and Flashlight Stun Guns

Rule 17

The 21-foot Rule

The 21-foot rule states that the average person with a knife or sword can get to and cut a person in about the same time that the average person can draw and fire a handgun.

21-Foot Rule: *In the time it takes the **average** officer to recognize a threat, draw his sidearm and fire 2 rounds at center mass, an average subject charging at the officer with a knife or other cutting or stabbing weapon can cover a distance of 21 feet.*

Don't assume that a gun is always superior to a knife. If you are within 21 feet of a knife fighting expert or martial artist with an edged weapon, the odds might actually be in his favor. Many knife fighting experts can cover up to 21 feet and cut your throat before you can draw your weapon and put it into play (think of the speed of Bruce Lee), especially if you don't have easy access to your holster. A knife is also generally more difficult to wrestle away from a suspect than a gun. Those of you who have seen episodes of the TV series *Justified*, will find great interest in this topic.

This is a very controversial topic in law enforcement and good arguments have been made on both sides of the fence; however, the bottom line which is rarely mentioned in police debates of this threat relates to RULE #2 (Warrior Mind Set) of this book. Your mind is your greatest weapon and if you are in condition WHITE, it is my opinion the odds of a bad guy winning the 21-foot rule with you are greatly increased.

Some of the noteworthy studies on this issue were conducted by Dennis Tueller of the Salt Lake City, Utah Police Department who wondered how quickly an attacker with a knife could cover 21 feet, so he timed volunteers as they raced to stab the target. He determined it could be done, on average, in 1.5 seconds. These results were first published as an article in SWAT magazine in 1983. A defender with a gun has a dilemma. If he shoots too early, he risks being charged with murder. If he waits until the attacker is definitely within striking range, so there is no question about motives, he risks injury or even death. The Tueller experiments quantified a "danger zone" where an attacker presented a clear threat. The Mythbusters TV series actually covered the drill in a 2012 episode "Duel Dilemmas", and their results indicated that at 20 feet the gun wielder was able to shoot the charging knife attacker just as he reached the shooter. At shorter distances, the knife wielder was always able to stab prior to being shot! Even if the person with a gun could shoot the person with the sword or knife before they get cut, the question remains whether or not the bullet would stop the person from cutting them.

This was a tactic used in the Philippines when the United States had control of the country. It is said that the U.S. Army switched to the .45 caliber pistol since soldiers under attack by people with swords were shooting them but not stopping them. During the American occupation of the Philippines in the early 1900s, Moros, marked by tiger-eyes and red headbands and sometimes under the influence of narcotics, conducted numerous suicidal attacks on U.S. troops with swords. Attacks similar to the Japanese Banzai attacks, embracing the belief that every slain Christian assured their places in heaven. The word "Moro" is a term for ethnic Muslims who lived in the Southern Philippines. So tenacious was the Moros' rampage that hundreds of reports by American soldiers surfaced, stating that the slugs of .38-caliber pistols failed to stop the advancing Moros. As a result of those reports, the .45-caliber Colt model 1911 semi-automatic pistol was specifically designed and issued to American servicemen.

Dennis Tueller retired with the rank of Lieutenant from the Salt Lake City, UT Police Department, taught at Thunder Ranch and International Training Consultants, the American Pistol Institute (Gunsight), International Association of Law Enforcement Firearms Instructors and more. He is currently with Glock Professional, Inc. as a firearms instructor and armorer. Mr. Tueller advised me in a recent interview that the term "21-Foot Rule" should probably be renamed with another title such as "Reactionary Gap" or "Proxemics" as the distance of danger cannot be exactly determined as 21 feet and depends on numerous factors. He stated, "There is no specific 'rule' to determine when deadly force is necessary or justified. I have never used the term '21-Foot Rule' as this is an issue of reaction and response time, not specific distances. 'Rule' has a nice catchy ring, but I think it is a very poor term. I would have never called it that. Your defensive tactics should be in response to what the circumstances dictate! What is your drawing time? With a high-security holster, an officer may take two seconds or more just to clear the holster."

In real-world encounters, many variables effect time, which is the key component of the 21-Foot Rule. How fast and agile is the suspect versus the officer being assaulted? What is the training skill, firearms expertise, and stress level of the officer? Is the suspect drunk, under the influence of drugs, or stumbling? How adept is the officer at drawing his holstered weapon? Is there any cover or obstacles between them? Is the officer uphill or downhill from the suspect? These factors and many others can impact the validity of the 21-Foot Rule, but the bottom line is that you are almost always better off to keep a significant distance between yourself and an assailant with an edged weapon!

Use extreme caution when you confront the mentally ill. You never know how they will perceive your comments to calm them down and your attempts to de-escalate the situation. They may be experiencing hallucinations and hearing voices that threaten them in ways you could never anticipate. Keep your distance to enable an adequate time to react.

Rule 18

Don't Underestimate The Threat Of Females And The Elderly

While the majority of psychopaths are male, they can also be female. Some of the best assassins in history have been females, because men tend to let their guard down when they confront a female suspect. Male officers are frequently reticent to conduct a complete and thorough frisk search of females to avoid accusations of improper behavior, until a female officer arrives to conduct the search. Remember Bonnie Parker? Keep in mind it only takes 2 pounds of trigger pressure to shoot some firearms. Some females and the elderly can shoot just as well as any well-trained male marksman.

Designer Concealed Carry? Old, but still DEADLY!

Left: Modified Pushup Bra with Holster Right: Compression Shorts with Hidden Holster www.undertechundercover.com

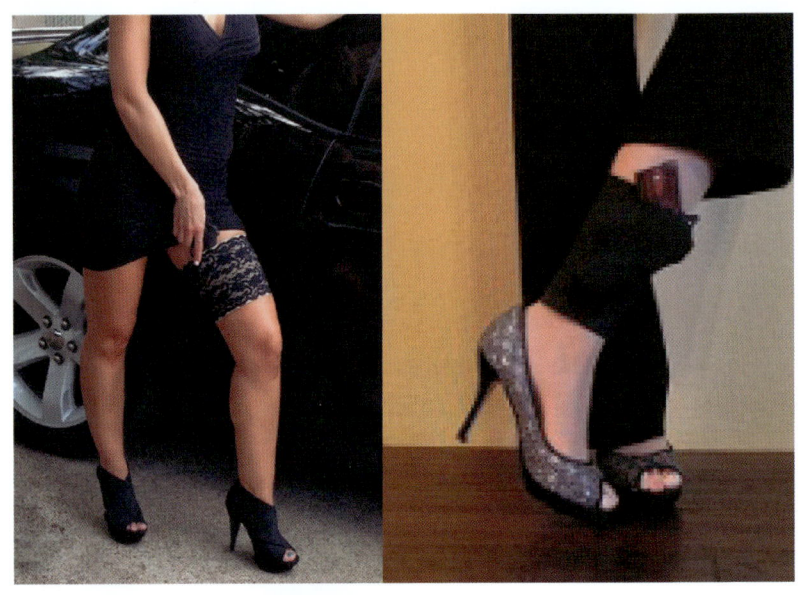

Top Left: Garter Holster
Top Right: Ankle Holster
Bottom Left: Corset Holster
Bottom Right:
The Lipstick Dagger - Another dangerous concealed weapon which can be purchased by anyone. This small dagger is frequently carried by prostitutes. Don't underestimate the danger of female suspects!
www.smkv.com
Photos Courtesy of www.femmefataleholster.com

Case Example

Letting Your Guard Down With Females Can Be Fatal to the Armed Citizen

A very dramatic shooting spree took place in Las Vegas, Nevada, on June 8, 2014. A married couple, identified as Jerad and Amanda Miller, ambushed and assassinated two Las Vegas Metropolitan police officers who were eating at a pizza restaurant on their lunch break. Jerad Miller espoused extreme anti- government views and posted several online videos in which he was dressed as the Joker from the Batman movie. Jerad shot Officer Soldo in the back of the head with a handgun and then shot Officer Beck in the throat. Both Millers then killed Beck by shooting him multiple times after he attempted to fight back. The Millers stole both officers' guns and dragged both the officers' bodies out of the booth they were sitting in, and covered Officer Beck's body with a yellow Gadsden flag and a swastika. The Millers loudly declared that this act was the start of a "revolution".

The second phase of this shooting spree took place when the Millers fled to a nearby Wal-Mart where Jerad fired a shot at the ceiling and ordered shoppers to leave. Joseph Wilcox, an armed citizen who was carrying a concealed weapon, drew his weapon and confronted Jerad, but did not consider Amanda a threat, and passed Amanda as he moved forward to confront Jerad. Wilcox did not suspect or realize that Amanda was armed and associated with Jerad. Wilcox probably assumed Amanda was just another female Wal-Mart customer and evidently didn't anticipate her as a potential threat when he walked by her. Amanda, thereby, had the drop on Wilcox and used this opportunity to shoot and kill him as he approached Jerad. Police later responded to emergency 9-1-1 calls and arrived at the Wal-Mart engaging the Millers in a gunfight, during which Amanda was wounded. Police moved toward the back of the store, where they tried to protect themselves from gunfire using several items from the store as a barricade. Police eventually shot and killed Jerad, while Amanda opted for suicide by shooting herself in the head and died from that gunshot. Las Vegas Sheriff Doug Gillespie described Joseph Wilcox as a hero, saying, "Joseph died attempting to protect others. His death is completely senseless." Wilcox's attempt at stopping Jerad Miller by using his concealed firearm also led to a debate over concealed carry, its effectiveness, or lack thereof, during similar incidents.

Rule 19

Don't Rely On Less Lethal Options

Photos courtesy of TASER International, Inc.

Pepper sprays (oleoresin capsicum) and CS gas are not always effective to stop an extremely aggressive or drug-influenced violent predator and may only give you a false sense of security. Non-lethal weapons are better than nothing, but the new TASER® conducted electrical weapon (CEW), or the ZAP cane stun gun (if you want to carry a cane), are the only less than lethal weapons I would recommend. I heard from many of my local police law enforcement colleagues that pepper spray and the CS gas sprays were very overrated, and I later discovered from my intentional personal victimization by these sprays that this was indeed the truth. Pepper sprays and CS gas are not nearly as effective as I had assumed them to be from the manufacturer's propaganda. When I attended the DEA Defensive Tactics Instructor School, many students were shot in the face with a heavy dose of CS gas spray from only 6 inches in front of our faces and the results were very mixed.

We did not volunteer for this unpleasant experience because we were masochists who enjoyed pain, but because we wanted to know for certain these sprays were truly effective before recommending them to any police officer. It is true that for about half of the students the CS gas was fairly effective at stopping them from being able to continue any aggressive behavior. One student would spray another student standing immediately in front of him with a heavy dose to see if the victim of the spray would still be able to rush at him and attempt to grapple with him on the FBI gym mats after being shot with the CS gas. Some of the participants did drop to the ground yelling in pain and grabbing their face. Some had to close their eyes and could not see, but there were a significant number who had no significant negative effects that would have prevented them from continuing to fight very effectively. I know I was in pain and I could not see near as well as normal. I did have to close one eye, which was heavily dosed, so I may not have been able to engage well in a boxing match, but I was still able to grapple to try to take the handgun away from my partner in the exercise. It didn't immediately knock everyone down to the ground as some had advertised. I do not think this was because the students who were still able to resist arrest and fight after they were sprayed with CS gas in the face were any tougher than the rest, it was just that pepper spray and CS gas tends to be very effective on some people, but have little or no effect on others. I do not mean to rain on the parade of all you young ladies who carry those CS gas and pepper sprays, but don't be certain they will always work. They might just really anger your adversary and make him want to beat the hell out of you. It is true, I don't think most men sprayed with a heavy dose of pepper spray would still be motivated to engage in rape with their face burning and eyes in tears, but many of them would still be able to fight and probably be very angry and, therefore, more likely to assault you.

Stun guns are reportedly more effective at stopping a violent aggressor than the pepper sprays, but the thing I don't like about most of them is that you have to get right next to the criminal and stick him with them. I don't like the idea of a potential female rape victim having to get that close, where she might have the weapon wrestled away from her. I much prefer the TASER® CEW, which shoots two barbs on a wire from a distance and which almost always incapacitates the violent predator. This allows the potential victim to shoot, then run, before the predator has any opportunity to get close to them. It is noted there have been a few rare cases where the Taser did not immediately work, and the suspect still attempted to grab the officer's handgun. I certainly don't recommend the TASER CEW to be utilized against a suspect who is pointing a gun at you, but if the criminal does not have a firearm, this appears to be a very prudent weapon to utilize. It incapacitates them, but rarely causes serious injury like a firearm and is therefore, an excellent tool for the police and potential crime victims to utilize when confronted by a suspect who is threatening and is not pointing a firearm at you. The success and relative safety of the TASER CEW is demonstrated by the fact that the vast majority of police departments in the country now carry them. When I was a young man watching the Star Trek movies, I remember how the "Federation" security personnel could put their "Phaser" weapons on "Stun", and thought about how great that was; well, I guess that day has finally arrived. If you are a hiker, or need to carry a cane, the "ZAP Walking Cane Stun Gun" might be a good, and less expensive option for you. It also works well to fend off aggressive dogs. It costs less than the TASER, but does not shoot two barbs up to 15 feet like the TASER. It can be extended to 36 inches to give you a little distance from your attacker.

I love the idea police and law-abiding citizens now have a middle option, and can now incapacitate a violent criminal who does not display a firearm, without having to shoot him with a firearm, or beat him with a baton, which could cause permanent serious bodily injury or death. When my daughters asked me if they should carry a handgun, I first asked them, "Do you think you would hesitate to shoot someone if your life was threatened and you were in fear of your life?" One of my daughters was very assertive and advised me that she was certain she could shoot if her life, or the life of a family member, was threatened. She took the firearms safety courses and now has a concealed carry permit. Another one of my daughters was a little hesitant in her response. She was not certain, but she did advise me she would not hesitate to shoot someone with a TASER CEW because she knew it would probably not kill them. Upon hearing this, I purchased a TASER CEW for her to carry in her handbag.

The TASER CEW is a great weapon for many women and men to carry who think they might hesitate to shoot a firearm. They can now use a TASER CEW to shoot a rapist or burglar, who doesn't have a gun, to protect themselves and their children and not have to worry about causing serious injury or killing anyone. How great is that?! It is also great for police officers who are frequently put in situations where they know they might get in trouble for shooting a firearm in some very dangerous situations, but can shoot a TASER CEW at a suspect who won't comply after several directives such as "show your hands, drop the knife, stop moving toward me, get your hands out from under the seat, etc.", or a suspect who just wants to fight with the police, but doesn't have a gun. It should be noted, that Taser utilization has resulted in death in a few extremely rare cases.

I believe those rare cases probably related to a heart problem of the person being shot with the weapon. The police officer with a Taser no longer needs to worry about a mandatory physical confrontation that might result in a death from the officer having his weapon taken away. Remember those statistics about the significant number of police officers who are killed with their own handguns when the unarmed suspect wrestled it away from them!

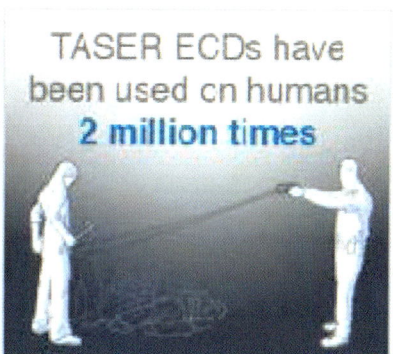

The probes deployed from a TASER CEW carry fine wires that connect to the target and deliver the TASER into his neural network. These pulses delivered by the TASER CEW overwhelm the normal nerve traffic, causing involuntary muscle contractions and impairment of motor skills. So, this naturally begs the question – if the TASER CEW output current is so low, how can it be effective in stopping a violent subject? The answer is because the TASER CEW current does not rely on brute force, or on sheer power. Instead, the TASER CEW pulsed output is really an elegant approach to incapacitating violent persons. The TASER CEW pulses mimic the electrical signals used within the human body to communicate between the brain and the muscles. The TASER CEW simulates the pulsed communications used within the nerves, and interferes with communication – like static on the telephone lines within the body.

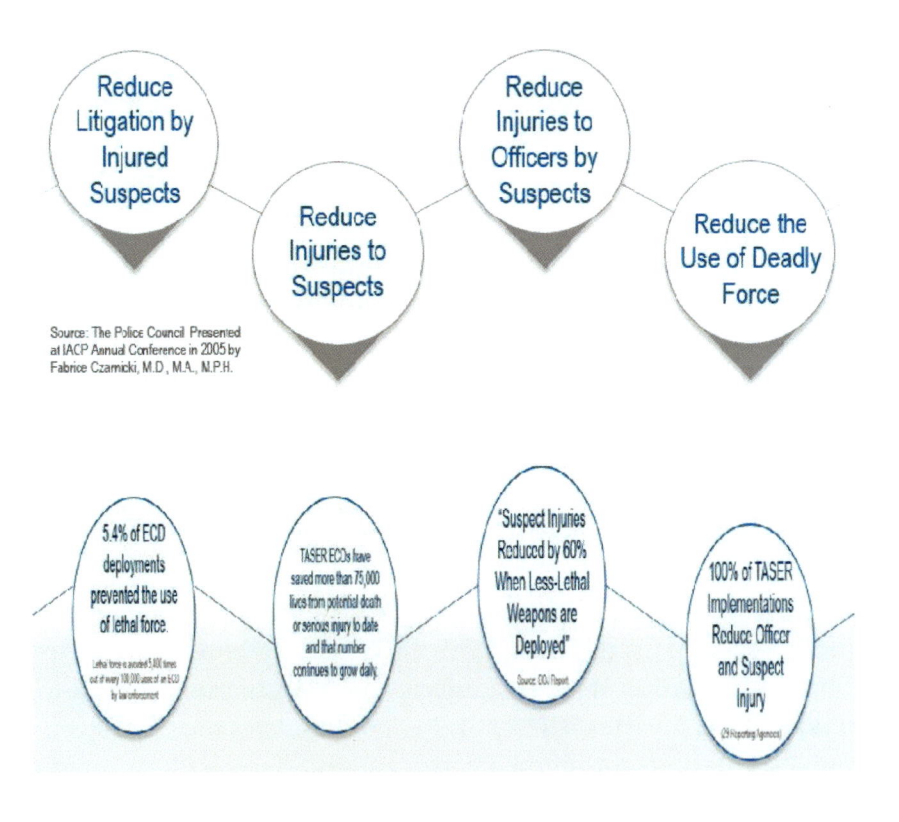

- Reduce Litigation by Injured Suspects
- Reduce Injuries to Suspects
- Reduce Injuries to Officers by Suspects
- Reduce the Use of Deadly Force

Source: The Police Council Presented at IACP Annual Conference in 2005 by Fabrice Czarnicki, M.D., M.A., N.P.H.

- 5.4% of ECD deployments prevented the use of lethal force. Lethal force is averted 5,400 times out of every 100,000 uses of an ECD by law enforcement.
- TASER ECDs have saved more than 75,000 lives from potential death or serious injury to date and that number continues to grow daily.
- "Suspect Injuries Reduced by 60% When Less-Lethal Weapons are Deployed" Source: DOJ Report
- 100% of TASER Implementations Reduce Officer and Suspect Injury (29 Reporting Agencies)

The added 15 feet of distance between you and an attacker is more than just space: it's safety. The farther away you are from an assailant, the easier it will be for you to escape the threat and prevent the situation from escalating to a more dangerous or harmful conclusion.

With the TASER CEW, LASER sights make aiming at a target simple and accurate. In addition to not relying on pain compliance, TASER devices are also effective in defending you only against your threat. Other personal protection options pose a risk to the victim as well. Pepper spray or MACE can backfire and also harm the defendant, putting them at greater risk of injury.

The Smaller TASER C2 CEW Is Also Available For Your Self Defense Needs

Key Benefits
- Knock an attacker out of commission and get away safely
- Take a mugger down…from up to 15 feet
- Same range and effectiveness as the law enforcement-grade models
- Integrated LED flashlight and laser sight for easy, confident firing
- Use as a 'stun gun' without the cartridge or after the cartridge is fired
- Compact enough to fit in your pocket
- No license needed to carry openly or concealed*

It is legal in the United States except in Hawaii, Massachusetts, New York, New Jersey, Rhode Island, and the District of Columbia. Additional cities, counties, and countries might have other restrictions on the use or possession of the C2 CEW so check all applicable laws and regulations carefully. Federal law prohibits carrying or shipping TASER devices out of the U.S. without the proper export license. TASER CEWs are not classified as firearms by the U.S. Bureau of Alcohol, Tobacco, Firearms, and Explosives (BATF) because TASER cartridges use compressed, inert nitrogen gas to launch the probes instead of gun powder.

Available in titanium, black, yellow, blue, red, and fashion pink.
Photo courtesy of www.taser.com

Rule 20

Modern Technology Makes Bullet Proof Equipment Very Effective

Ballistic shields, helmets, and bulletproof vests are extremely effective and have saved the lives of numerous law enforcement officers. Why not utilize them? In the middle ages gunpowder made the heavy armor of the knights on horseback obsolete and body armor was abandoned for the most part in recent history in view of the penetration capability of high powered firearms, but technology has now evolved to the point where body armor for police officers and soldiers is now relatively light weight and very practical. Most high quality ballistic vests will stop virtually any handgun or shotgun round, with the exception of some types of special ammunition designed specifically for the penetration of ballistic vests.

Technology has also developed some ballistic shields and bulletproof vests that will even stop many high powered rifle rounds, but they are usually very heavy and cumbersome to maneuver with on the battlefield. Police officers conducting raids in the future will probably look like the old Roman Centurions or Vikings in a shield wall formation marching forward with locked shields for protection. Few violent criminals wear bulletproof vests, but be prepared to shoot to the head if you suspect they have body armor.

Although officers know the benefits of wearing soft body armor, many still choose not to wear it. Officers often complain about the comfort, fit, and breathability of the vest, especially in the warmer months. Research has shown that between 1980 and 2001 approximately 1,200 officers have been killed in the line of duty. More than 30 percent could have been saved by body armor. The save percentage is even higher when evaluating felonious assaults involving firearms. It is estimated that the risk of dying from gunfire is 14 times higher for an officer not wearing a ballistic vest than for one who is (Source: Police Chief magazine). I know of at least one DEA Special Agent whose life was saved by wearing a ballistic helmet and another saved by utilizing the ballistic shield shown below. I am glad to see police now also use ballistic vests to save our K-9 buddies!

Rule 21

Relaxing Too Soon

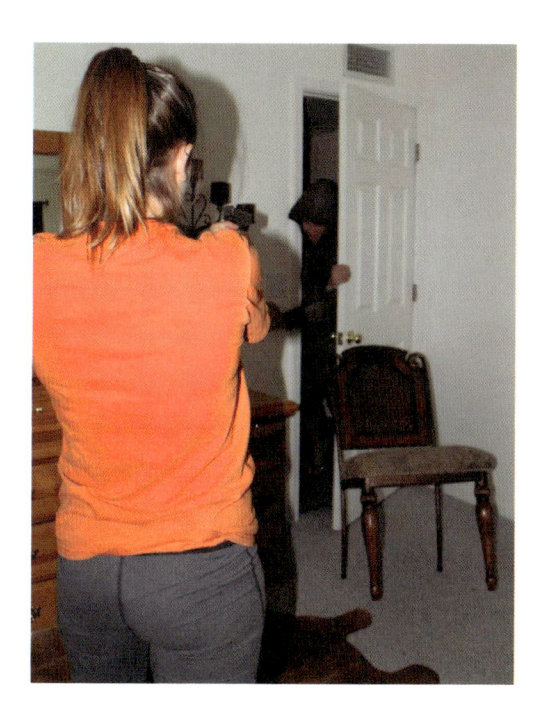

Never relax too soon and assume the threat is over! It is rare, but even fatally wounded suspects have occasionally recuperated their physical capabilities, after being shot several times, long enough to kill police officers who let their guard down and did not think to immediately handcuff and search them. Also, do not let yourself get into the "rut" of false alarm calls, and thereby, let your guard down. Just because you answered the same alarm call at the same location a dozen times before and it was a false alarm, doesn't mean that can't change. Observe the activity, never take any call as routine or just another false alarm. Police officers frequently become complacent while performing the same functions day after day. This is the mindset which can get you killed because each call, no matter how similar in nature to the previous call, has its own unique set of circumstances.

This concept of "relaxing too soon" also applies to the armed civilian. Sally was a very attractive woman who had been stalked by a suspicious male for several months. She was so concerned about his prowling around her house that she obtained a concealed carry permit. One day, when she came home from work, she observed that a small window on her front door was broken and suspected a burglar or rapist may have obtained entry. She was smart enough not to go inside and waited outside, with her hand on the gun in her purse, until the police arrived. When the police arrived, they conducted a quick walk through of the residence and observed no one inside and no property missing. Sally and the police **assumed** it was probably just a random act of vandalism. Sally went back into her house alone, after the police departed, and put her purse with the gun in the bedroom and started preparation for dinner in the kitchen. Approximately 10 minutes later, the rapist/ burglar emerged from the bed he was hiding under in the guest bedroom, and Sally became the victim of rape. The police and Sally both relaxed too soon and did not check out every possible hiding place in the residence. Observe carefully. Are you certain the crisis is over? Don't be quick to relax simply because the immediate and apparent threat has been neutralized. It's your life on the line.

Another very vulnerable location for rape is large parking lots after dark. If you are being followed, cross the street and walk toward a crowded area while you call the police. It doesn't cost you anything to call them and report a suspicious person. If you are walking toward your car, have your keys already in your hand ready to quickly open the vehicle, lock the doors, and start your engine for escape. Many women have become victims of rape because they dawdled and lingered in front of the car door or front door to their house digging through their purse searching for keys they could have already located while walking toward their home or vehicle for quick entry. Entry to your vehicle or home by a rapist can provide a location for rape where you cannot be seen, or screams for help heard, by pedestrians walking nearby. Some women carry a whistle or loud alarm device of some type in the hope someone might hear the alarm if they are assaulted and a good Samaritan or police might then come to their assistance. I see little value in these types of alarms. People hear car alarms go off every day and very few people search out the source of the alarm to investigate. I also speculate that a woman screaming for help would be more likely to draw attention than a whistle or beeping alarm.

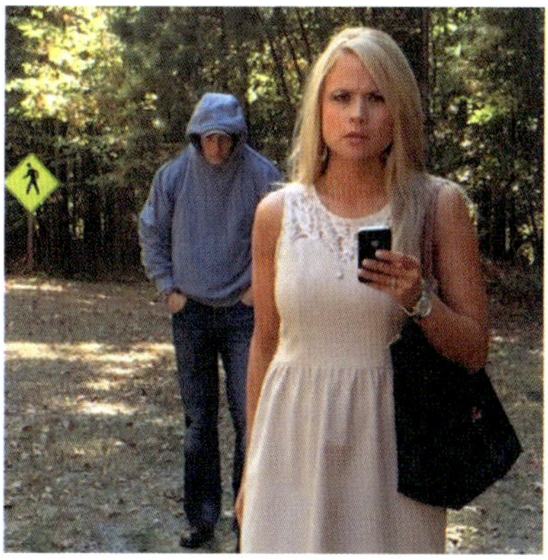

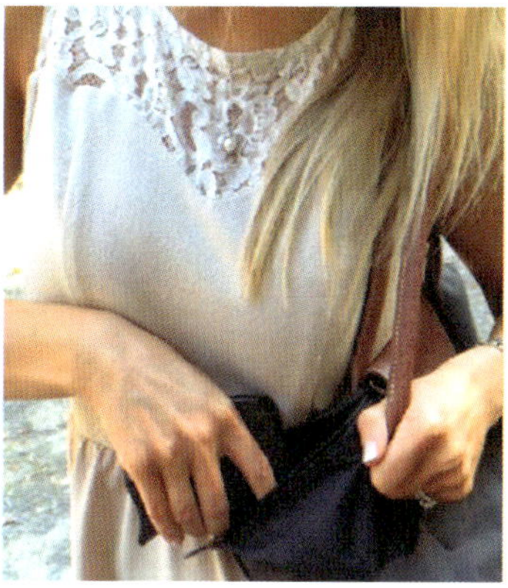

Case example

Why You Should Never Relax And Not Be Vigilant With Stalkers

A Las Vegas woman's ordeal with a relentless stalker finally came to an end when he invaded her home. Fox 5 Vegas **reported** on the shooting of a man who tried to break into his ex-girlfriend's home. The unnamed woman chronicled her terrifying experience with a stalker who harassed her for over six months. Turning to the social networking site, Reddit, in search of help, she posted:

> *"For the past 6 months I have been relentlessly stalked and had threats against my life made from someone I dated for a month. It started with phone calls upwards of 45-50 a day, 50 page text messages and him showing up outside of my house at 5 am. When I wouldn't comply or feed the negative attention I began to receive threats, claims that he would murder me and get away with it, all he would have to do is flee the country. Telling me he shouldn't have to force me to be his friend or give him another chance or else. Every time I blocked his number from contacting me, he would then call me from different ones, try and pretend to be other people or have his friends or sometimes even random strangers he'd ask on the street…"*

The frightened woman relocated, but this didn't stop her stalker:

> *"Mid July he created a profile using my photos and likeness to threaten my family, when I didn't respond he proceeded to post semi nude pictures of me on the profile in attempt to black mail me into speaking with him. I did not and contacted TWITTER to report the account and have it removed which they eventually did. On 08/21/2014 I awoke around 8pm to vigorous knocking and ringing of my doorbell. I look out my window to see who it is and I was horrified to see my stalker there. I called the police and of course he fled once again (over 7 separate police reports filed). This incident was followed by threatening emails from my stalker demanding that I meet him somewhere or because he had found me that next time I would "wake up to gun-*

shots" and that if I didn't he would first "taser you and rape you in the a** using your boyfriends blood as lube."

Police weren't able to do much to help the situation:

> "This past Sunday night I woke up at 6:45 am. to the ringing and banging again, I proceeded to recorded him on video while I was on the phone with the police. He fled on foot once again and I was hit with the same hoopla from law enforcement "Well we can't really do much because technically at this point he's not doing anything wrong."

Upon obtaining a temporary restraining order against her stalker, the woman asks Reddit for help in getting a private investigator to locate her stalker's residence so he can be served. Sometime after soliciting Reddit for help finding a private investigator, the woman shared an image to Imgur along with a startling update to her story:

> "I'm writing this staring at the mess the police left for me, in a bit of a fog. After 6 months of stalking and threats against my life my stalker finally snapped and decided to kick my door in and make good on his promise. Out of fear, the past month I had begun sleeping with a chair propped against my front door, to give myself a few extra precious seconds in case of emergency. I shudder to think how differently things might've turned out had I not barricaded the door. I awoke around 1:15 am to the sound of the door giving way after one kick followed by the sounds of my stalker struggling to dislodge the chair while forcing his way inside. I jumped up and grabbed the gun I've learned to do everything even shower with. I stood at the top of my stairs and fired twice. Hitting him in the chest, I hear his scream, his disbelief that I'd stood up for myself. 0 to 100 in milliseconds. I've never been so afraid in my life. I do not know if he is living, but I do know the police have him and that's what helps the most. For months of him evading the police I began to question whether he was unstoppable? Untraceable? Houdini? He would murder me and get away with it? As of now I'm in a haze of guilt, surprise, relief and disbelief. I shook as the canines drag him out from his hiding

place under a bush. I survived, where so many people do not. Holy shit, I survived…"

Never forget the importance of vigilance and home security. Dogs and alarm systems might give you some warning you have an intruder in your home, but little things like remembering to keep your doors locked, or putting a chair up against your bedroom door, can sometimes make a big difference. This woman had developed the warrior mindset and did not hesitate to use deadly force when it was necessary, and it saved her life. The police will not always be there immediately when you need their help. Be prepared. Be vigilant. Be a survivor!

Summary

The 21 Deadly Rules Of Gunfight Survival

1. **Preparation & Safety:** I know it is only common sense, but the first rule to survive a gunfight is to have a gun. Will you have ready access to a reliable weapon when you need it? If your weapon and ammunition are separated and/or locked up in a safe, glove box, or trunk of your car, you probably won't have time to obtain it before you are assaulted! Nonetheless, if you have children in your home your paramount concern should be to make certain they do not have access to your firearms. If you have children, a good practice is to have only one loaded pistol stored in a combination lock briefcase on a very high shelf in your bedroom closet.
2. **Mindset:** The "Warrior Mindset" to be able to recognize a threat and respond appropriately is just as important as your accuracy with a firearm. Remember that your mind is your most valuable and powerful weapon!
3. **Take Advantage Of Cover If It Is Available:** Remember to always take advantage of cover (trees, barricades, walls, car doors, etc.) when you draw your weapon. It will be much more difficult for your adversary to hit you with a bullet if the only target area exposed is your gun hand and dominant eyeball for sight picture.
4. **Triangle Of Skills:** The triangle of gunfight survival is a mixture of the survival mind set, movement for cover and tactics, and firearm marksmanship accuracy.
5. **Target Aquisition:** Knowing where and how to shoot a violent criminal to stop an attack. The caliber and magazine capacity of your weapon is not as important as the reliability and easy access of your weapon and your marksmanship capabilities with it. Multiple shots may be required to stop some violent criminals and a shot to the "Triangle of Death" is the only shot which will immediately stop a violent deadly threat.
6. **Stress And The Unarmed Suspect Is A Killer:** The STRESS of a life and death confrontation will destroy

your firearms accuracy if you are not mentally prepared. You need to develop muscle memory that makes shooting your firearm an instinctive reaction via extensive training. If you have to think about it, you might hesitate, and hesitation means possible freezing under stress.

7. **Flinch Will Destroy Accuracy:** Flinching while shooting is the cause of most accuracy problems. You must engage in dry fire firearms practice on a regular basis to force your mind and body to be positively conditioned to not have the muscle memory "flinch" reaction to a loud explosion when you are shooting your firearm. Shooting live rounds actually conditions your mind and body to expect and anticipate the recoil of your pistol and may cause you to "flinch". Dry fire practice has the complete opposite effect on your brain and should therefore be conducted even much more frequently than live fire training.

8. **Firearms Shooting Fundamentals:** If you do not want to take the time to learn how to be proficient with your firearm, it might be better for you not to have one, as pulling out a weapon you are not skilled with could result in having it taken away from you, or become the tool of your own demise. You must learn and PRACTICE, PRACTICE, PRACTICE all of the proper techniques of muscle memory proper stance, footing, handgun grip, arm & elbow lock, breathing techniques, and sight picture. Remember to always squeeze the trigger and the only part of your body to move when taking a shot should be the smooth movement of your trigger finger to avoid barrel wiggle. You need to teach your body to remain completely stable once the shot breaks. Once you have memorized it properly, it is like riding a bicycle and you will not forget how to do it.

9. **Weapon Advantage:** Rifles and shotguns are superior to handguns and are more accurate, especially in long-range gunfights, and have better stopping power than most pistols. Just as you wouldn't bring a knife to a gunfight, if you have a choice, don't bring only a pistol if your adversary has a rifle or shotgun.

10. **Tombstone Courage, The Dirty Harry Syndrome:** Don't develop the "Dirty Harry" syndrome and try to be the Lone Ranger. Whether you are a civilian who has just found their house broken into, or a police officer responding to an emergency, always call for police backup and never enter a building alone to confront a suspect by yourself, unless mandated by exigent circumstances.
11. **Never Give Up:** Never give up the fight or your gun! There are exceptions to every rule, but I have seen few circumstances where giving up your weapon and surrendering, because the bad guy had the drop on you or you ran out of ammunition, resulted in a positive outcome. Depending on your distance from your adversary and the ability to run behind cover, you might be better off to take your chances and simply run like hell than surrender, as moving targets are much more difficult to shoot with a pistol.
12. **Proper Distance:** Maintain proper distance to keep your weapon out of reach of your adversary. Distance is usually in your favor, especially if you are a small female confronting a large male suspect. Never forget that even 8% to 10% of the trained police officers killed in the line of duty were killed with their own guns when the unarmed suspects managed to wrestle their pistols away from them.
13. **Reliability Of Weapons & Equipment:** Is your equipment reliable, tested, and well maintained? Never bring an untested weapon into battle! For civilians this probably only means your firearm and possibly a flashlight and cell phone, but for police and the military it includes a wide variety of support equipment such as handcuffs, radios, flashlights, batons, Tasers, etc. Having the battery go out on your flashlight in a dark building with a burglar, because you forgot to change the batteries, could become as dangerous as having your firearm jam during a gunfight.
14. **Handgun And Caliber Selection:** The .45, .40, and .357 Sig caliber semi-automatic pistols definitely have better stopping power than a .22, .25, .32 or .380 caliber pistol,

but if the large calibers cause you to flinch and miss your target you might be better off with a small caliber pistol. The bottom line is that the caliber of your pistol is not as important as your accuracy with the weapon. A .22 caliber round which hits your adversary between the eyes is much better than a .45 caliber round that missed him. Pick the caliber and handgun you can be accurate with.

15. **Proper Holster Selection:** Just as you select a pistol which has good stopping power, but more important, you know you can shoot the most accurately, select a holster based on comfort and practicality. It doesn't really matter how it looks. The question is whether you will wear it every day. There is no limit to holster makers' inventiveness. There are numerous types of gun vests, pouches, and holsters. Many gun owners have a drawer full of holsters at home they will never wear again. Find your ideal holster. If you are not comfortable with your holster, keep looking until you find the right one you will wear every day. If you are not comfortable, you will not wear your gun. A gun left at home may be as useless as having no gun at all!

16. **Never Assume Anything:** Never assume your adversary is unarmed and does not have back-up or hidden weapons! Even if the suspect is handcuffed he can still pose a significant threat, especially if he is a kick boxer or mixed martial artist. Always handcuff suspects with their hands behind their back and always keep your eye on them, even if they are handcuffed. Never trust the search of a fellow police officer and always conduct a thorough search yourself of every suspect taken into your custody. Police officers and military personnel have been killed by trusting a previous search as the prisoner pulled a hidden weapon not discovered.

17. **21-Foot Rule:** Don't assume that a gun is always superior to a knife. If you are within 21 feet of a knife fighting expert or martial artist with an edged weapon, the odds might actually be in his favor. Many knife fighting experts can cover up to 21 feet and cut your throat before you can draw your weapon and put it into play, especially if you don't have easy access to your holster. A knife is

also generally more difficult to wrestle away from a suspect than a gun.

18. **Don't Underestimate The Threat Of Females And The Elderly:** Some of the best assassins in history have been females, because men tend to let their guard down when they confront a female suspect. It only takes 2 pounds of trigger pressure to shoot some firearms. Some females and the elderly can shoot just as well as any well-trained male marksman.

19. **Don't Rely On Less Lethal Options:** Pepper sprays, CS gas, and stun guns are not always effective to stop an extremely aggressive or drug influenced violent predator and may only give you a false sense of security. Non-lethal weapons are better than nothing, but the new TASER® conducted electrical weapon is the only less than lethal weapon I would recommend.

20. **Modern Technology Has Made Bullet Proof Equipment Very Effective:** Ballistic shields, helmets, and bulletproof vests are extremely effective and have saved the lives of numerous law enforcement officers. Why not utilize them?

21. **Relaxing Too Soon:** Never relax too soon and assume the threat is over! It is rare, but even fatally wounded suspects have occasionally recuperated their physical capabilities long enough to kill police officers who let their guard down and did not think to immediately handcuff and search them.

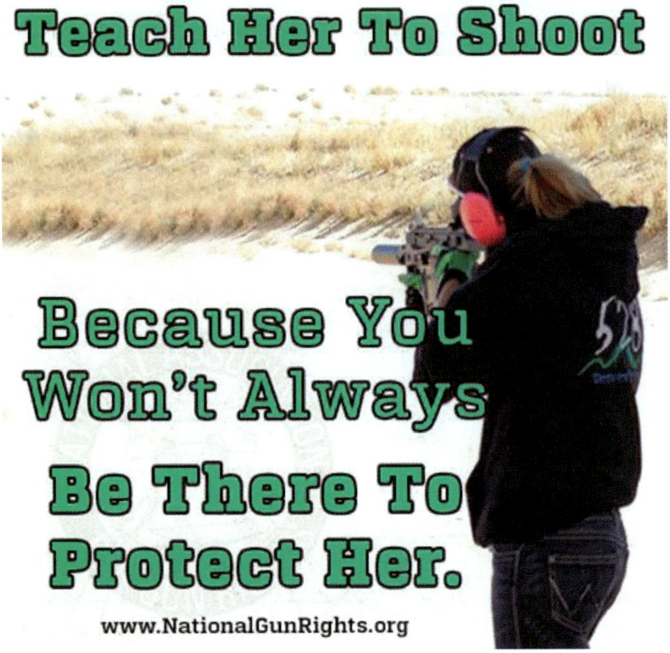
Teach Her To Shoot
Because You
Won't Always
Be There To
Protect Her.
www.NationalGunRights.org

Closing comments

You are NOT for **WOMEN'S RIGHTS** when you want to strip them of THEIR RIGHT to **SELF-DEFENSE**

The famous quote "All men are created equal" is perhaps the best known and most frequently quoted short phrase of Thomas Jefferson in the U.S. Declaration of Independence, but are all men really created equal? We should all have equal rights, but some of us certainly have greater physical defense capabilities than others and this is why the 2nd Amendment to the U.S. Constitution is so important. When an old lady in a wheelchair has a handgun, she has as much power to defend herself against criminals as a muscleman like Arnold Schwarzenegger. One study showed that as many as 200,000 women use a gun every year to defend themselves against sexual abuse. The firearm is the true equalizer of power, justice, and self-defense capability! I believe the old saying, "God made man, but Samuel Colt made them equal," originated as an advertising slogan for Colt Manufacturing.

History has shown us that strict gun control is one of the first measures enacted by tyrants in modern history. The three biggest regimes of genocide in world history (Mao Ze-Dong, Jozef Stalin, and Adolf Hitler) all immediately enacted strict gun control measures to insure an unarmed population that would be unable to resist their control and diabolical plans for genocide. Historians estimate the regime of Mao Ze-Dong killed over 30 million of his own citizens during the Communist Cultural Revolution in China. One study estimated Jozef Stalin killed over 7 million Russian and Ukraine citizens (gulags and purges, plus the Ukraine famine), but I have seen some estimates that as many as 20 million people were killed by Stalin's policies. If this is true, the infamous Adolf Hitler would actually be rated #3, behind the two communist purge tyrants. It is estimated Hitler killed 12 million people via non- battlefield or combat deaths (concentration camps and civilians deliberately killed in WWII plus 3 million Russian POWs left to die).

In contrast, the armed American citizen with the Kentucky rifle was empowered to confront and defeat the most powerful military in the world at the time of the American Revolution, the British Empire. The so-called "Assault Rifle" is the modern equivalent of the Kentucky rifle of the 18th Century. Some gun control advocates contend that low magazine capacity rifles, shotguns, and pistols (10 rounds or less) are the only firearms which should be allowed for the law abiding citizens to protect themselves from crime, even though there have been some reported crime incidents (although rare) where more than 10 rounds were needed. It is the gun control advocates contention there is no need for assault rifles or firearms with high capacity magazines to protect yourself from criminals. They also contend that the idea that U.S. citizens with small arms, such as assault rifles, could stand up to any modern army with air power and tanks is ridiculous. Therefore, they hold the opinion armed citizens might have a justification for small magazine capacity firearms in relation to protection from crime, but in view of modern air power and modern weapon technology such as drones, helicopters and tanks, the armed citizen is irrelevant in regard to national security and the protection of liberty from tyrants, domestic or foreign, with a modern army.

In response, it is noted the insurgents in Afghanistan have seized few tanks and have no air force whatsoever, but appear to have kept the two most powerful military powers in world history, both Russia and the United States, from taking control of their country with primarily only small arms resources. The Taliban certainly has no tank divisions of which I am aware. Though vastly outgunned and outnumbered, the insurgents have waged guerilla warfare in the countryside and find sanctuary in remote mountain regions. I would suggest that proponents of this idea that a guerilla army with small arms cannot possibly prevail against a modern army should take a look at the Nicaraguan Revolution and Afghanistan's history, and view the film Red Dawn for a visualization of how this could be accomplished. As mentioned in the Introduction, historians believe Hitler did not invade Switzerland because he knew every able-bodied young man in the country had been issued a rifle and knew how to shoot. The Viet Cong also had no air force and few, if any tanks, but were able to keep the U.S. Army at bay long enough for the North Vietnamese army and air force to enter the fray in greater force and eventually win the conflict. It was not until the final Vietnam conventional campaign in 1975 (when US air power had vacated the field) that tanks and heavy batteries were openly used in Vietnam in significant numbers.

"PoliceOne.com" recently conducted the most comprehensive survey ever conducted of American law enforcement officers' opinions on the topic of gun control. More than 15,000 verified law enforcement professionals took part in the survey. Virtually all respondents (95 percent) say that a federal ban on manufacture and sale of ammunition magazines that hold more than 10 rounds would not reduce violent crime. The majority of respondents (71 percent) say a federal ban on the manufacture and sale of some semi-automatics would have no effect on reducing violent crime. About 85 percent of officers say the passage of the White House's currently proposed gun control legislation would have a zero or negative effect on their safety, with just over 10 percent saying it would have a moderate or significantly positive effect. The overwhelming majority (almost 90 percent) of officers believe that casualties would be decreased if armed citizens were present at the onset of an active-shooter incident. More than 80 percent of respondents support arming schoolteachers and administrators who willingly volunteer to train with firearms and carry one in the course of the job. More than four in five respondents (81 percent) say that gun-buyback programs are ineffective in reducing gun violence. While some officers say gun violence in the United States stems from violent movies and video games (14 percent), early release and short sentencing for violent offenders (14 percent) and poor identification/treatments of mentally-ill individuals (10 percent), the majority (38 percent) blame a decline in parenting and family values.

The author of this report, Doug Wyllie, is Editor in Chief of PoliceOne. Chief Wyllie concluded the report with the following statements, "Contrary to what the mainstream media and certain politicians would have us believe, police overwhelmingly favor an armed citizenry, would like to see more guns in the hands of responsible people, and are skeptical of any greater restrictions placed on gun purchase, ownership, or accessibility. Quite clearly, the majority of officers polled oppose the theories brought forth by gun-control advocates who claim that proposed restrictions on weapon capabilities and production would reduce crime. In fact, many officers responding to this survey seem to feel that those controls will negatively affect their ability to fight violent criminals. The officers patrolling America's streets have a deeply- vested interest — and perhaps the most relevant interest — in making sure that decisions related to controlling, monitoring, restricting, as well as supporting and/or prohibiting an armed populace are wise and effective. With this survey, their voice has been heard."

The recent Sandy Hook Elementary School shooting in Newtown, Connecticut, where Adam Lanza fatally shot 20 children and 6 adult staff members, has rejuvenated efforts to ban high magazine capacity firearms, especially assault rifles, in the United States. In reality, the largest death toll in an assault on a school did not involve an assault rifle, but a bomb. The Bath School disaster took place in Bath, Michigan, on May 18, 1927, killing 38 elementary school children and 6 adults and injuring at least 58 other people when school board member Andrew Kehoe set up a series of explosions in the Bath Consolidated School. Kehoe also detonated his shrapnel-filled vehicle outside the school. The bombings constituted the deadliest act of mass murder in any type of school setting in U.S. history and clearly show you do not need firearms to conduct mass murder. Bombs were certainly illegal in 1927. What makes gun control advocates think that making assault rifles illegal would solve this type of problem, when bombs have always been illegal and did nothing to prevent this terrible tragedy and numerous other mass murder bombing incidents such as the Boston Marathon or Oklahoma City bombings? The 9-11 terrorists reportedly utilized box cutter edged weapons, not firearms, to hijack airlines and kill 2,996 innocent Americans. Would making box cutters illegal in the U. S. really do anything to help solve the problem of mass murders?

Firearms are not a mandatory item for mass murder or even mass genocide. The Rwandan Genocide that took place in 1994 killed an estimated 500,000 to 1,000,000 Rwandans and the vast majority of victims were not killed with firearms. The Rwandan government recruited or pressured Hutu civilians to arm themselves with machetes, clubs, blunt objects and other weapons to rape, maim and kill their Tutsi neighbors and destroy or steal their property. If the minority Tutsi had owned a significant number of firearms to defend themselves, the number of deaths might have been reduced significantly, and the mass genocide might possibly have been avoided entirely.

While on the topic of minority rights in relation to gun control, it is noted racially discriminatory gun laws existed in the American colonies even before the American Revolution. Just like the genocide regimes of the modern era who utilized gun control to prevent resistance to their unjust "final solutions", lawmakers in America enacted statutes barring slaves from possessing firearms. That ban was often applied equally to free blacks, who enjoyed most other rights, lest they join in an uprising against the slave system. Where blacks were allowed to possess arms, as in Virginia in the early 1800's, they had to first obtain permission from local officials. Trust the government, as they know what is best for you!

Photo courtesy of Smoky Mountain Knife Works www.smkw.com

In conclusion, history has shown us that strict gun control has frequently been a precursor to human rights violations, and those who ignore history are doomed to repeat it. I believe convicted violent felons should not be allowed to own firearms and criminals should receive severe prison sentences for crimes committed while in possession of a firearm, but laws which prevent law abiding citizens from owning firearms will only serve to increase, not decrease, the violent crime rate in our society. To quote an oft-cited phrase, "When guns are outlawed, only outlaws will have guns!"

Printed in Poland
by Amazon Fulfillment
Poland Sp. z o.o., Wrocław